A Dead Man Lives In
Detroit

But It Ain't Over Yet

Allen Bennett

Allen Bennett
beruandal@aol.com

Printed in the United States of America

E-mail: beruandal@aol.com

ISBN-13: 978-1467928984

ISBN-10: 1467928984

Library of Congress Cataloging-in-Publication Data

Printed in the United States of America

Editor: Rebekah Pierce

Available in paperback and e-book.

Dedication

This book is dedicated to the memory of those who did not live to write or even read this story. Many of them could probably have done a much better job.

Acknowledgments

I acknowledge the mercy of Jesus first for the undeserved privilege to write this book. Secondly, I acknowledge my wife/friend Beverly for her ever encouraging words, "I got your back baby."

Table of Contents

Introduction ix
Chapter 1: *Childhood – Part I* 11
Chapter 2: *Childhood – Part II* 18
Chapter 3: *Home* 35
Chapter 4: *Rage* 48
Chapter 5: *I Challenged God* 50
Chapter 6: *Detroit Riot 1967* 54
Chapter 7: *Detroit Homicide* 58
Chapter 8: *First Degree Murder was the* 66
Sentence they gave me 66
Chapter 9: *Going Back* 80
Chapter 10: *Role Models* 87
Chapter 11: *Peek-a-boo With Death* 97
Chapter 12: *Chief of Fools* 101
Chapter 13: *A Different Side of Allen* 103
Chapter 14: *Homeless* 111
Chapter 15: *1996 - The Darkest Hour* 121
Chapter 16: *COMAYA Ministries* 126
Chapter 17: *My Beverly* 141
Chapter 18: *Grover* 160
E P I L O G U E 171
About the Author 173

Introduction

Drugs and substance abuse made a slave of me for over twenty years. This life caused me to be pronounced dead the minimum of three times. I was ultimately homeless. Can a person who was a pimp, thief and murderer be chosen by God for His service?

This list only describes some of the despicable hats I wore, yet God's mercy and grace freed me. I pray that by sharing the gory details of my miserable past others may receive deliverance. Jesus died for everyone; even me! My disgraceful past has been erased. I am forgiven.

Chapter 1: *Childhood – Part I*

Throughout my childhood, I would go into what I now know to be a depression about twice a year. During these times, I would ask my mother certain questions. BB is my mother's nickname. These episodes dated from age eight or nine until my early teens. I would go into a mode where I would want to stay in the house. Because of my love for the game, I became very good at shooting marbles. I had so many marbles that I would sell marbles to other kids. During my episodes of depression, while I stayed in the house, I would usually go to the couch in the living room to practice my marble shooting. During these episodes, that is all I wanted to do.

At other times, I would listen to music. I would lie on the floor in front of the record player and just listen to music. Nobody in the family had a clue how to address my strange behavior. I guess they just said I was a weird kid. I probably was. When I did speak during these times, I would talk to my mother. I would ask her these kinds of questions. "Why do I have to go to school and grow up and get a job and get married and have kids and pay bills and things"?

I wanted to know why I would have to go through all of these changes just to die. But what I was really asking her was what was the meaning of life. I was asking my mother questions that throughout the ages had been asked by men regarded as being more wise than myself. These questions were not really so peculiar, but they were like dropping an atomic bomb on a poor, ignorant, uneducated black woman from Alabama who was struggling to make ends meet for her family. I would ask her these kinds of questions and her answer would always be religious sounding. She really didn't know. At times, I would pressure her to the point of compelling her to say that she really just didn't have answers. That being said the conversation would end until my next episode of depression.

In 1975, at the age of twenty-five, I was serving a life sentence for 1st degree murder. I was transferred from Jackson Prison to the Wayne County Jail awaiting the next phase of my appeal process. The Michigan Supreme Court had declared my life sentence null and void.

One day the guards took the prisoners to an outdoor recreation period. We were taken outdoors to a basketball court. While there, I was called by a woman standing near the fence. She was accompanied by a young man. She called my name again. I looked at her trying to see if I knew her and I said, "I'm sorry?"

She told me that she was my mother. I had not seen her since her release from the hospital. She had undergone a triple operation involving her gall bladder among other complications. She had lost nearly 50 pounds. She had changed so much that I didn't even recognize her; my own mother. My cousin Larry was standing beside her. She told me that she had something to tell me, but that she couldn't tell me right then. She emphasized that as soon as she could, she had to tell me something very important. At that point, they took us inside. I was released on appeal bond a month later. My appeal bond release was pending my scheduled second trial on the murder charge.

Leading up to the time that I was brought to the Wayne County Jail, I was in very close communication with the woman who is now my wife, Beverly. We corresponded daily in letters and over the phone. A few months before I was brought from Jackson to the county jail, Beverly had received the baptism of the Holy Spirit. All our plans for marriage were put on hold. I wasn't yet fully aware that our plans had actually been cancelled pending my commitment to live for Christ. I did recognize that something was wrong, however. Our plans had come to a sudden standstill. We were in strife constantly.

This was basically the circumstance of our relationship after Beverly had accepted Jesus as her personal savior. The fire of God was so ablaze in her life that He affected my mother too. One week after Beverly's baptism, my mother was baptized as well in the Holy Spirit. Shortly after my mother's deliverance, Shirley (my sister) became Spirit filled. The woman who would become the mother of my two sons was ministered to by Beverly at my mother's home. She too received the Holy Ghost. I had no idea when my mother called to me from the fence that day that she had accepted the call of Holiness for her life.

I was released on an appeal bond in July of 1975. Alas, I now had the time to talk with my mother. We sat down and she explained to me that she had never forgotten all of the times over the years when she had wanted to give me answers to my questions but couldn't. She told me that the answers she couldn't give me all of my life to those hard questions were answered in a man named Jesus. She told me that she had just found them out herself. She had received His Spirit and the wisdom that was coming from feeding on His Spirit was developing within her. His new life in her was the answer to all the questions I'd asked her as a little boy. In her heart and mind, she had found the answers. Her need to share her discovery with me was rooted solely in the love of a mother for her son.

She was excited and eager to tell me about Jesus after having met him for herself for the first time. It was visibly a great victory and relief for her. But for me, it only cast me deeper into a state of turmoil and confusion. You see, the one woman that I believed truly loved me for myself - the only woman that I wholeheartedly was committed to loving for the rest of my life - had received this thing called the Holy Ghost. To top it off, the only other person in the world that I trusted without question was my mother and now she too had received this Holy Ghost. I felt this Holy Ghost was infecting people all around me; the people closest to my life. This Holy Ghost had really thwarted my plans to just come out of prison and continue my gangster life with Beverly as my wife. My plans were obviously out the window. Little did I know, God had His own plans!

For a number of months, I tried to identify with what Beverly was going through, but living two lives with each pulling me in opposite directions caused us to eventually separate. We were forced to experience just what kind of fellowship light really has with darkness. None! So, we went through the motions for awhile with good thoughts in our heads and love for each other in our hearts. But being drawn away by the mediocre gangster life I was living, which Beverly had no knowledge of, our efforts to be together proved to be in vain.

In the chapters that follow, you will witness up close what I call my flipping, flopping, tripping, falling, and stumbling through life to ultimately end up in the arms of Jesus. He is now my savior. In these chapters, my prayer is that my experiences will serve God's purpose by detailing my route to a place of salvation and deliverance. I eventually arrived at a place of knowing or as one pastor said, "At a place in my life where I knew in my heart that I had arrived at the place that I should have been all of my life. I know that I am where I belong."

I know that I am home now. I have a measure of that peace that passes all understanding. In spite of any circumstance, I now have a confident measure of God's peace in the midst of a storm. I know that when the dust settles, I will have the peace of God in any situation. God's peace has literally kept me for over fifteen years.

This book merely describes in some graphic details the extent of my confusion. You will read about a lot of the pain, a lot of suffering and a lot of the tragic consequences of sin. I just did not know or believe. I am not ashamed to blatantly and vividly display my ignorance of the word of God. I read the Bible before my deliverance for almost thirty years without having an understanding of what I was reading. But I thought I understood.

Though there were many scriptures I always remembered, I never opted to make the transition from having a mere head knowledge of the word to having an understanding of the wisdom required to apply it. I never recognized a real need to ever want to understand. I understand now that wisdom must and can only come from God. God must empower a believer by anointing us to understand and become a doer of the word and not a hearer only. I didn't have this empowerment. I associated the word of God and what I thought of as religion as two different things. What I witnessed in the lives of so-called believers seemed unrelated to the God that I read about in my bible.

I was never really inspired, motivated or encouraged to make a connection between what was written in the Bible and what was to be practiced on a daily basis in my life. People talked about it and I heard about it, but I really never saw anyone ever actually practice a lifestyle that would even come close to provoking me to Godly jealousy for the word of God and the things of God.

The pages of this book will reveal the ramblings of how this man/boy found his way to Jesus. How I found my way to a place where I knew that only God's mercy had answered my life's dilemmas . I remember sitting in that hallway in my last drug treatment center trying to trick the very people that were trying to help me.

Their job was to help me find relief from active worship of the dope demon that had robbed me of nearly twenty-seven years of my life. These people were trying to help me through a treatment program that had apparently been founded by a former addict who knew how to stop using dope. If I would follow the steps of their program, active drug addiction would no longer be a part of my life.

I know a number of people who are free of active drug addiction because of this program. But there is no man-made program in the universe that can relieve a man from the oppression of spiritual bondage, guilt and shame. No one and nothing can give us what we need to fight Satan but our acceptance of God's forgiveness by and love of God. The devil's spirit is alive and is operating in the earth. Apparent evidence overwhelmingly proves his existence and influence. Just look around! There is so much evil going on in our midst that is out of control. There is so much happening, that nobody wishes for, that nobody could ever want. Only the author of confusion - the spirit that is out to steal, kill, and destroy us all could want this mess.

You will see that I have journeyed to some very ugly places. Many memories are still very painful to recall. One potential benefit of writing this book is that my tragic experiences may be a lamplight to someone. The Lord may privilege me to be a ray of hope to someone who is yet in the midst of this terrible demonic oppression, this slavery, this same attack from the enemy as I was. I offer these glimpses into some very shameful areas of my life for the purpose of helping someone. I have been helped by so many people that were used by God to make this day possible. There are many people who have helped me whose names I don't even know and may never know.

Chapter 2: *Childhood – Part II*

I was born in Bessemer Alabama in 1949. My earliest memories are of living in a home where corn liquor "moonshine" was sold. We lived in Alabama until I was five years old. As a small child, I can remember playing with some of the people that came to our house to buy liquor. I particularly remember one drunk we called Sarge. He sang the blues while playing the guitar with me on his knee. I must have been four years old. I can remember the police raids of our home. Expecting to be raided at anytime, my mother would hide the liquor in the chimney stack. This maneuver kept the cops from finding it while still allowing our customers easy access.

I would sometimes go to the graveyard at night to retrieve the liquor reserves my mother and stepfather hid in five gallon steel containers. I remember being afraid at night in the graveyard. I remember being with my mother in the car in the dark in the graveyard going to get the liquor. On one occasion, the police caught us in the graveyard, but my father was the only one arrested. Sometime that same night, my mother took me with her to pick him up from jail.

I called my stepfather Dick. In the wee hours of the morning, we sat in the car in the dark waiting for his release. I can still remember how scared I was. Dick was released from custody through a back door of the jailhouse. When I could clearly see that it was him coming down the steps, I was so happy. Looking back, trying to analyze the whole situation, it's not hard to see how I developed a negative attitude towards the police. This attitude became blatantly manifested in many ways later on in my life. My mother told me that the reason we left Alabama in 1955 was because she refused to pay the police.

We were making more money than most of our peers. The difference in how we lived in comparison to everyone else became quite conspicuous.

My mother and stepfather had an unquenchable thirst for making money. They also were in total agreement about saving their money. My mom was a very good hustler. She was very proprietary. She knew how to handle common people well and I learned how to handle them from her. My father was a very hard working man. He was also doggedly persistent in pursuit of almost anything he believed would produce dollars. He made a lot of money, but not without consequences that were quite costly later on.

One of my last memories of Alabama is when we were moving to Detroit. I was five years old and I owned a tricycle. I remember sitting outside our house on my bike as we were moving. I turned my tricycle on its side. I was playing with one of the wheels pretending I was driving to Detroit. Somebody had said we were going to Detroit. My father was an over the road truck driver. He had gone to Detroit and made arrangements for our family to have a place to live.

I don't have a whole lot of memories of Alabama beyond being in that house with all of the drunks. I can only see now how things were happening inside of me that would impact my entire life. These memories mark my beginnings, but their far reaching effects are showing up even today.

In 1955, we came to Detroit. I was the oldest of three children at the time. My sister Shirley was two years younger than I. My youngest sister, Savannah, who we called Nookie, was two years younger than Shirley. Savannah was the only biological child of my mother and stepfather at the time. My sister Shirley was raised as Shirley Harris. She was, however, never officially adopted by Dick. The deception concerning Shirley's last name caused her some growing pains later. It was especially traumatic for her when, as a teenager, she found out that her name was really Shirley Bennett.

Prior to her birth, she was used as leverage by my mother to get away from my biological father. By all accounts, my biological father was not a good provider. I don't know how my father found out about my mother's affair, but I have heard that he was known to be very prone to violence. I will not judge if her adultery and deception was not well deserved. I am told that during our time together as a family, we actually experienced hunger because of his squandering of money and his parading himself about town as a big shot. In their little world, my father's family was looked upon as having a little more than most of their neighbors. I have never really looked into this to see what impact this might have had on my mother. I do know that she used to laugh and jokingly describe how she used to beat up my father as a child. This was not uncommon for my mother. She is the only person that I have ever heard of who never lost a fight. I have heard that she did do a lot of fighting. In fact, I adapted a lot of her ways that I can see today.

At a very early age, she suffered severe burns in her stomach area. AS a small child wearing a highly flammable nightgown she was burned severely when the burning nightgown stuck to her. She was burned so badly they didn't expect her to live at one point. She was also never expected to be able to sustain child birth. Though all four of her babies were delivered by cesarean section, she had four live births. I thank God for that.

Something about her upbringing in that cultural environment in Alabama put a deep defense mechanism in her. She has a bit of a mean streak. In her culture, she was looked upon as being cursed since it was thought that she could not bear children. My mother was a mean fighter, but she was also a loving and giving person. But if and/or when a person ever violated her trust, anything could happen.

I was like that myself before Christ. I remember the first night we arrived in Detroit. We were lost about a block from where we were supposed to be living. That night was the first time I ever saw a street car. It was frightening. I could see the sparks from the connection cables on the top of the street car. I was horrified. Of course, as I look back now, I can also see another aspect of my character developing even then. While I was a mortally afraid five year old kid from Alabama, I was also sensitive to the fact that my sisters were more afraid than I. They were shaking and crying. I believed that it was my duty to protect them, so I hid my fear. I was the oldest and at five years old I was trying to protect them.

Another memory stands out in my mind from Alabama. There was a little boy on our street that I used to play with. Sometimes he wanted to fight, but I would never fight him back. My mother would get very angry at me. She would say that I should stand up for myself; that I shouldn't let him beat on me like that. I knew in my heart that I just didn't want to hurt him. I was not afraid of him.

I am not sure if I just finally reacted to my mother telling me to fight back, but one day I did fight him back. I hurt him severely; bad enough for him to go to the hospital.

The word around the neighborhood became that I was a mean, bad kid; that I was crazy. My feelings were hurt. In tears, I told my mother that I hadn't fought him back because I didn't want to hurt the little boy. I asked my mother why he always wanted to fight when I just wanted to play. She could not answer. I understand now that there are some people that are extremely sensitive to the pains of others. These peculiar or empathetic individuals can actually feel the pain of other people. I was like that as a child. I could feel their pain if I inflicted pain or perceived the suffering of pain by another person. It is hard to describe, but that's how I once was. It would physically hurt me to know that I was hurting someone, and often I would rather suffer pain at their hands than to hurt them in retaliation. I felt that I was forced into doing what I did to that little boy.

As life went on, though, I eventually reached a time when I felt nothing. There came a time when I was the exact opposite of the little boy I am describing. I thank God my life didn't end in that condition. But yet, I can now identify a perverted remnant of that evolved condition when fifteen years later, I took a sawed-off shotgun, walked up to a man and told him that I had come to kill him. I told the man in that hallway that we were indeed going to rob them, but I wanted to kill him, and that is exactly what I did. I aimed the sawed-off shotgun at his chest and I shot his heart out. I remember that on the day that I took his life, I felt the same feeling that I felt when I beat up that little boy. In both cases I wanted to render the ultimate hurt.

22

Our first temporary residence in Detroit was a two-family flat occupied by the family of one of my mother's brothers. This brother was one of two that preceded our arrival in Detroit. Both prided themselves as macho black men. Since they were somehow favored by the women, they produced a lot of babies by different women. This shared flat was the home of one of those women. My mother's brothers opportunistically exploited my parents monetarily because they didn't know their way around yet. We lived there for a few months pending the purchase of our home a few blocks away.

I have mostly painful memories during this short period. On the first floor lived the family of a woman with eight children. Two of the children were in our age group. One of them, Priscilla, was my age; she liked me. There was also one brother a few years younger than Priscilla. The other siblings were older in ages ranging into young adulthood. Their habit was to tease my sisters and I; our southern accent sounded funny to them.

They teased Shirley because of her short hair and negatively compared her looks to Nookie. (They thought Nookie looked better than Shirley.) They teased Nookie because of her light complexion and they teased me because of my speech impediment. I stuttered uncontrollably.

I was a constant laughing stock to them. I could take my ridicule in stride since the kids that were doing this were all larger than me. I couldn't win and I knew it. But I would not accept what they were doing to Shirley. I had to stand up for her. So, I gained their respect because I would fight everyday for Shirley and lose every day. I can still remember the way that I felt inside fighting for Shirley. I still have that passion, but it manifests in different ways today.

I soon identified the two siblings that I could control; the youngest boy and the girl. While the older ones would taunt and tease Shirley, I harassed their younger siblings in their absence. If they were going to mess with Shirley, then I would mess with their siblings. The girl wouldn't fight me back because she liked me, but I would taunt her and make her cry.

Within six months, we moved out of that place into a house a few blocks away. I was glad to be away from those people. Most of them were so much bigger than me. I daily fought a losing battle, but I fought nevertheless. I was so unhappy there.

Schooldays rolled around. My mother took me to school the first day. On the second day, my mother was preparing to return with me to school. I asked her what was she doing and she told me that she was taking me to school. I told her I knew the way and that she didn't have to take me. That is another thing that I remember and appreciate about my mother. If I told her that I could do something, she would trust me to do it. She would try me. I learned a lot about life based on that principal and my mother's trust. I thank God for my mother.

I went to school the next day alone. Most of the kindergarten students were accompanied by their parents. I had learned to read in the Alabama pre-school. I must have learned a lot because it soon became apparent that I was more advanced than my classmates. I was more advanced in most areas in the classroom, but I had a problem with stuttering.

I was mistakenly regarded by a few of my teachers as not

having very many smarts. They contacted my mother and told her that I couldn't read. At the same time, I was getting the highest grades on all of the written material. One day, my mother came to school and asked how could I get the best spelling grades in the class, but yet not be able to read? My mother couldn't understand that. She was not able to present her point acceptably to the school administrators, so things continued on as before.

I have always enjoyed academics. I love to learn and I like to read. As I grew older, I remember becoming so compromisingly yielding to peer pressure that I would not pursue academic excellence. I wanted to belong and to feel accepted by the group. It was not considered a good thing to be the smart kid. Therefore, my reaction to the threat of social ostracism caused me to hold back. I didn't want to be that different. I can remember times when I wanted to step out and pursue my greatest capability academically, but would lose heart.

In short order, my father got together with some people and started making corn liquor again. It quickly developed into a thriving business such that it wasn't long before we conspicuously stood out from our neighbors in our tiny little corner of the world. Everyone could see that our family had the material things they could only wish for. This difference lasted throughout my childhood. We appeared as rich kids in comparison to the lifestyle of our peers. Whatever they had, we had more of it and ours was better than theirs.

This separation caused me to not have many close friends. I can only remember one person that I really considered my friend. I now remember him with mixed feelings. We met when I was about seven; he was a little boy, maybe three or four years old. He used to use the toilet in his clothes. He was the little fat boy who the kids used to bully and harass. His sister was my age. She had a light complexion and freckles. They would bully her also since she was afraid to fight. I became their avenger by stopping the bullies from bothering them. That was the initial point of contact and it sealed a lifetime bond.

I also stopped the bullies from messing with his sister. By young adulthood, she imagined that she was very much in love with me. It didn't turn out to be anything. Her brother and I became very close friends. Our close friendship lasted throughout most of my adult life, but after my release from prison, the differing paths of our lives forever changed our relationship. Things between us have never been the same since.

In most other ways, my childhood was not that different from other kids in the neighborhood. A certain core group of neighbors had contact with our family since our home was the meeting place for the people that drank corn liquor. People would party at our house on weekends. Our home was a rendezvous point for those having adulterous affairs, but our house was not a whore house. On only one occasion did my mother allow her brother to co-habit with one of my playmate's mother. The woman lived as the wife of their stepfather. She and my uncle were not supposed to be there together, but my mother did let them have sex in our house.

The other time was when my mother was entertaining her boyfriend there. I never saw them in any sexually compromising way, but I did see a man other than my father being catered to in ways that should have been reserved for my father only. It was inappropriate enough for a twelve year old boy to see that something was wrong.

We were selling liquor by the gallons and were considered "big shots" in the hood. My parents saved money well. They also both worked outside the home. Neither parent was formally educated beyond grade school, but my father was functionally illiterate. His jobs were always menial and very physically demanding. He finally secured permanent employment in a barrel reconditioning factory. Starting at the lowest level, through hard work and sacrifice, over the years, he became the supervisor.

He was a very hard working man. He held his position as supervisor for over twenty years. When the factory closed, he was offered a job at another place nearby based on what they had heard about his work at the barrel reconditioning factory. He held that position until he retired.

These memories describe the more memorable parts of my childhood leading up to where I am now. I liked to dance. I liked to roller-skate. I tried to be what I considered a regular kid. I liked to dress sharp, but I always wanted to be the sharpest dresser in the crowd. I always wanted to know what was the best of any particular style. When I learned what it was, I wanted that item only. I wanted to wear the best shoes and I would not be satisfied with anything less than the best.

In our home, crime was an acceptable means to an end. A job was regarded as a front. It was just a cover - a necessary hazard of making money. However, overt acts of violence were frowned upon. It just wasn't cool. I could sell liver –

27

consuming liquor and/or dope all day long. We sold stolen merchandise regularly, but, to us, that was just business. Prostitution and gambling was alright as well as anything else that came up. If we could make money with it, it was acceptable. We were game to sell anything except people and that was only because we didn't know how to buy and sell humans and get away with it. This is the way that I grew up.

This principal was reinforced by the people who came across the path of my life. I would transport bottles of liquor hid inside my pants for delivery to the parents of my playmates. We also became the numbers people in our neighborhood: My favorite aunt became financially stable by running numbers. I used to even carry numbers for my mother. I would come home for lunch in elementary school and would pick up the numbers. My chore while returning to school from lunch break was to drop the numbers off at Miss Jackie's house.

Miss Jackie's house was next door to our first residence in Detroit. Perry was one of Miss Jackie's sons. He met his death by drowning in a canal down by the Detroit River.

Miss Jackie had bought a big yacht with the wealth accumulated through taking numbers all those years. Perry got so drunk he fell off the yacht and was crushed between the dock and the boat. Prior to that, he was my childhood nemesis. Our fighting skills obviously must have been closely matched. We would fight for awhile and then were friends for awhile. This went on until we were teenagers. I particularly remember the last two fights.

One fight was on the side of the Catholic Church. Perry slugged me so hard that I fell and bumped my head. A big hickey developed right between my eyes. I was so ashamed. All the kids teased me. It took about two weeks for me to recover, but then we went at it again. I won this one. He had me pinned against a tree we called a cigar tree. It was dark and we were fighting just beneath the street light. As he was chocking me, somehow his finger got within biting range. I bit his finger and he started screaming.

He dropped his guard, unable to fight back. I kicked his butt for real then where everyone could see it. Everyone thought that I was a really bad dude that night.

Perry and I never fought again. I did, however, protect his little brother in the penitentiary years later. Some guys were going to rape him. He was a small person and had no friends in prison that would fight for him. He later became a maniac. He did something really vicious to a little child and he went crazy; he just went nuts and did some unmentionable abuse to the child of a woman he was living with. Again, these were the kinds of people that I grew up around.

Our family moved from the first upper flat to a house just a few blocks away. I felt like an outcast. I was rather puny in comparison to most of my playmates, but somehow it seems that I always found a way to go up against the biggest bully. It seemed like the only people that I could have friendships with were the girls. But it worked out pretty good, so I am not complaining.

When the parents of my playmates got into financial crisis, they would come to us to borrow money and/or pawn things. I can easily recognize now how some envy and resentment directed towards our family was passed from the parents to the children. I was never attacked directly. Most of the jealousy and resentment was taken out on my sisters, in particular, Shirley. I would always retaliate with viciousness and without restraint. I would treat them like strangers. I believed it was my duty to stand up for my sisters. I grew up with that attitude. This was my mindset and I can only now wonder how much of my childhood struggles were brought on by me.

I looked down on most of the parents of my playmates. I believed that my family was somehow above them. My parents never drank alcohol or gambled until the late 1960's. I was about thirteen years old when my father started drinking and hanging out with the guys. Not long afterwords, my mother started drinking too. I remember when my father learned to gamble. He became a very proficient poker player. We used to host weekend-long poker games. My father won a lot of money. He also learned how to cheat real well, and my mother worked in conjunction with him. She was the bar lady and she used to pinpoint certain men and feed them excessive amounts of liquor. This, of course, enabled my father to take advantage of them and win their money. That is how we lived and that is what we did.

Eventually, it all came back. My mother became an alcoholic consuming over a quart a day according to her own account. She used to carry a quart of liquor in her purse for back up. She carried a gun and thousands of dollars in cash every day. I used to do that too, so I know where I got that practice.

My father was nicknamed "Cigar" among his peers. He used to buy very expensive cigars and he dressed in high style according to our culture. People thought he was a sharp dresser, for some reason. I may have identified with that trait without even knowing it since I too love to dress well. Hopefully, it is without the same measure of flashiness.

My mother became an elegant woman of style. Having a more extensive exposure to contemporary style, her dressing habits befitted women of a higher social standing. She favored furs and expensive jewelry as we came into contact with a lot of expensive items of clothing via of our illegal connections. I sometimes ask my former neighbors how I was thought of. The consensus is that I was "aloof" - someone who thought they were better and didn't want to be very close to them. To my shame, it was the truth. We ostensibly had more material things than almost all of our neighbors and we flaunted it. If only they had been able to see how impoverished our hearts were.

When I was nineteen years old, I bought a Cadillac convertible. At that time, it was unheard of in our neighborhood. The girls came, sometimes two at a time.

On one occasion, two sisters said that they wanted to be my women. That sounded okay to me. As it turns out, one of them would be murdered by her husband who was a Vietnam veteran. When she decided that she wanted to be a part of my life, she began giving me all the money that he was sending home for her and her three children. Home from Viet Nam, he discovered the whole truth and he murdered her. The police stopped him while he was driving around with her dead body in the car. They saw him stopped at a red light talking to her dead body, bleeding from her temple with a hole in her head. He was released after three days because of post-traumatic stress disorder from Vietnam. I sadly acknowledge my contribution to her untimely death.

People in my neighborhood did not neglect any opportunity to steal from us. Many things that occurred around our property would not have occurred if we had had a more congenial relationship with our neighbors. In 1966, the FBI raided our home. During their preliminary investigation and while under surveillance, we were able to dismantle an entire liquor distillation operation on the third floor of our home. (My mother permanently damaged her knee while helping to carry a garbage can full of corn mash.) We had a coal furnace in the basement, so we were able to conceal the parts of the liquor still in the midst of the ashes from the coal furnace. We took the full garbage cans to the garage like regular garbage. We knew we were under surveillance.

In the garage, we put the cans in the car. My father took the garbage cans to his job and disposed of everything. When the feds raided our house, the liquor still was gone. During the preliminary investigation, I was put under surveillance and because of it. I have had a federal dossier since I was sixteen years old.

Sometimes I think of that day when the cops came in. No one was home but my mother and I . We joked with each other while the FBI looked for the elusive liquor still. As one agent went into a certain part of the basement, I asked, "Are you going back   there?" I told him that there were rats in there. He said that he didn't mind and I told him that he shouldn't. I told him that he and all the agents were of the same species as rats and they shouldn't be afraid. I was expressing anger towards the FBI agents for doing their duty. The apparent connection between that incident and my life experience as a whole - beginning years before as a child in Alabama - is undeniable.

Some years later while I was in Jackson Prison, I was charged with being in a cell with a homosexual. This was not my M.O. (modus operandi). The guard that charged me was looking through a gun tower hole. Because he was looking down from an angle, the officer thought he saw me exit a cell with the homo. I knew both the queer and the guy that was in the cell with him, but they were two doors down the gallery from my cell. Because of my commitment to being a thoroughbred gangster, I couldn't tell on them even at the cost of taking the fall for them. So, I did take the fall. I went to the hole - a solitary confinement cell - for two weeks. The guards from the cell block came to the disciplinary hearing and intervened on my behalf. They spoke up for me because they said they knew that I would not do that kind of thing.

In my childhood, the cops were regarded as enemies. During the raid in 1966, while my mother and I were expressing our distastes for their efforts, one FBI agent told us that we really shouldn't be mad at them. He told us that we should be mad at our neighbors for the more than twenty calls they had received about our illegal operation. He said that it was only because of our neighbor's complaints that they had investigated and subsequently raided our home We took that as a wake-up call and kept a relatively low profile until we moved out of that neighborhood. I didn't have a lot of fun in that neighborhood. How much of that was because of me, I don't know. There were some fun memories, though mostly they were of my music.

I always loved my music - jazz and rock and roll. Like most

other kids, I knew all the words to every Temptations and Stevie Wonder song. My particular musical niche became the jazz of Wes Montgomery. I called "Bumpin on Sunset," by Wes Montgomery, my theme song. Prior to my involvement with any kind of drugs, I loved my music. In my neighborhood, it was not cool for a young black man on the eastside of Detroit to admit to liking Frank Sinatra. But even now, I still love my classical music.

Chapter 3: *Home*

Our home was first and foremost a business place. Most mornings before we went to elementary school, my job was to serve drinks to the alcoholics. I was about nine years old. Some of the more extreme alcoholics required a drink in the morning just to get the shakes off of them. Without their morning "wake-up," they couldn't function the rest of the day. Often after their first drink, they would go out onto the porch and vomit, if they made it to the porch.

I used to measure out 50 cent shots of corn liquor in a half pint milk bottle filled up to the wavy line. A half-pint sold for a buck. The pint measurement we used was a store bought liquor container. We sold pints of corn liquor for $2. I also helped my father deliver the gallon orders at night. So, I developed a close attachment to our customers. I knew them as real people. They were special to me. I never thought of them as alcoholics, and I surely didn't consider the fact that we were helping to kill them. We made liquor that was so strong that if you accidentally spilled it on a wooden table, it would eat the varnish or paint right off of it in minutes. I can only imagine the damage it must have done to their livers. Most of our customers were dead long before I reached adulthood.

From age seven or eight, I had to keep the fire in our coal furnace going during the winter. Sometimes, I would have to get up in the middle of the night to make a fire. This happened whenever I had not prepared the fire properly to last throughout the night. I became really good at it as time went on. When the fire did go out, I would have to go outside, cut wood and make a new fire along with my usual chores. For obvious reasons, during the winter months, nothing took priority over the fire. I did just like I assumed any other obedient kid would do. It was just another part of my responsibilities like serving the drunks.

Basically, I had a lot of responsibility. I was given full authority over my sisters. I was able to discipline them, including using corporal punishment. I was like their surrogate parent. I loved them and I did not abuse my authority over them. Most of the conflicts that I had as a child with the other kids in the neighborhood were because of my sisters, in particular my youngest sister, Savannah. She was considered the pretty one and she had a big mouth. She was a real scaredy cat and wouldn't fight. I always had to come to her rescue. I had complete responsibility for their conduct in the house while my parents were gone. If the girls did anything wrong, it was understood that I would receive punishment for it. I received some beatings because of them.

Unfortunately, my youngest sister learned how to manipulate the system enough where she got away with a lot. I had to suffer the consequences for her bad behavior. I grew up believing that I was supposed to be held responsible for their wrongdoings. I can remember going to school in the winter once. None of us had gloves and it was very cold. My sisters were crying. Unable to think of anything else to do, I removed my two pair of socks to allow my sisters to use them as gloves.

There was another occasion I remember on the way to elementary school in very cold weather. On the corner opposite our home, there was a steep incline in the last couple of squares of the pavement approaching the curb. I was so little that I couldn't climb this incline and I had a nasty fall. I was hurt and crying, but by the time I got home, I hid my tears. I didn't want my mother to see me crying. The next day, it was still cold and icy. My mother happened to be looking out the window as I approached that same corner. She saw me as I crawled up the incline. Reaching the curb, I stood back up. She asked me about it when I arrived at the house and I told her that I had fallen there once, but I would not fall again. That attitude continued as I matured. I developed a policy that nothing and no one would ever hurt me twice.

In my elementary school class there was a girl who liked me. She and I had a gym class together, but something I can't remember occurred between this girl and I that angered me. Our gym teacher was a very muscular Caucasian man. I remember him as a man that was bald on the top of his head. I decided that this teacher thought too much of himself and I would break him down. I saw vanity in him and I wanted to prove to myself that it was true. At the same time, it seemed like a convenient opportunity to hurt the little girl too. So I came up with a scheme to make him do what I wanted him to do.

I told a lie on this little girl. I told the gym teacher that this girl was talking about him real bad. I told him that she was talking about how he wasn't really as strong as everybody thought he was. I told him that I just wanted to know if what she was saying was the truth. He called the little girl into the office with us and confronted her. He starting showing her his fists and flexing his muscles. This man was probably in his thirties; a grown man.

Notwithstanding, he utterly humiliated this little girl to prove to me in front of her that she didn't know what she was talking about. I immediately thought about what a fool he was, but I never thought about what an evil thing I had done. A pattern of manipulation and revenge marked my personality early.

Some of my teachers were sometimes seen at my house drinking and partying on the weekends. That made for even more strained relationships with both my teachers and peers. I was negatively affected in ways I am only now beginning to understand. To think about a lot of that stuff now gives me even more occasion to thank God for Jesus.

Another unfortunate circumstance in our home was that I became the default referee between my mother and father in their violent conflicts. In an attempt to get some perspective for my own peace of mind before writing this book, I called my sister and I asked her why were our parents always fighting. She didn't know either. These fights, for reasons I don't remember, became usual activity almost every weekend for at least ten years. I was in elementary school when it all started.

If the fight had not escalated into physical violence by the time I arrived on the scene, my mother, who was usually the aggressor, would launch her attack. My objective would be to get between them because neither one of them would hit me. My father was a man of about 6 foot 2 inches and in very good physical shape. My mother was obviously no match for him, but she was the aggressor 90% of the time. On most of these occasions, the only kind of blows from my father would be in defense of my mother's attack. She was very quick to find objects to use as weapons. She wouldn't normally grab a knife, but one time she did shoot him.

On another occasion, she found out that one of his tenants was paying her rent with sex. My mother wounded him on the top of his head. He needed stitches, but didn't get them. I cut his hair around the wound, cleaned and bandaged it. I look back sometimes and I think about what all of that was doing to me inside. I know that these experiences were not good and they must have left some deep scars.

I also never remember sitting down at a table for a family meal - ever. Our home was a business place. The kitchen table was used for serving alcohol. The dining room table was used for gambling more than anything else. My sister Shirley and I came to refer to our life at home as "drama." We would always say that the direction we wanted our lives to follow would be one that would never include a lot of drama like our childhood home. I did, however, eventually live through a period of drama that made my childhood home-life seem like child's play. My life became a nightmare contrary to my childhood vow. There were all kinds of fights between my parents.

As I said before, for some reason, they usually happened on the weekends. My mother was very money conscious and she would manipulate people all the time. We would buy and sell almost anything and we didn't care where it came from. If we could use it or sell it, we would buy it and people knew it. We had all sorts of goods and merchandise.

My mother was a consummate entrepreneur. She was also a homegrown "cornbread" psychologist. She was an expert in how to deal with people with a sole interest towards making money. She knew how to make money off of people which was her sole interest in them. I grew up in a home where the overriding consideration in most matters was measured against the question, "What's in it for me?"

Our ongoing profits were usually generated by the bad things that people liked to do. We were their "convenient proprietors." Even though what they usually liked just happened to be bad for them, we would, nevertheless, if at all possible, find a way to provide it and sell it to them. This was not just alcohol. Selling drugs for me was a normal progression of the lifestyle that I had been raised in. We sold clothes, hot cars - anything. We dressed the role according to what we thought was appropriate in our culture. We made an appearance at all the right functions; we looked the part. We mimicked what we considered socially prestigious. I talked the same talk as any other kid on the block. I can clearly see now, in hindsight, aspects of my character and personality that contributed to a lot of the carnage that I witnessed in my life later on. This was what the real drama looked like.

All these things were going on throughout my teenage years. In our little world, we considered ourselves among the sharpest dressers, the smoothest talkers and the best dancers. We somehow thought of ourselves as being a step above hard core jitterbugs, though we were jitter bugs too. We would go to parties and we would want to dance, but we wouldn't dance because the cool guys didn't ask girls to dance. The girls asked the cool guys to dance and that is the identification that I had. I wanted to be the "go to" guy. I imagined myself to be the guy who was a step above the common man. If I wore jeans, I wanted my jeans to somehow be different. If anybody needed anything, I wanted them to need to see me to get it.

Some of my teachers tried to reach out to me. One French teacher commented just before my high school graduation that she was happy that I was going to college. My original plan was to attend Wayne State in Detroit. She said that she feared that if I remained in the neighborhood, who knew what would happen to me. In other words, I would be one more casualty of my environment if I didn't escape soon. She was partially right. Unfortunately, the catastrophe turned out to be much worse than she probably ever dreamt. I would experience a living hell before Gods mercy would save me from me.

A few other teachers reached out to me to no avail. One of the premier musical choir directors in the Detroit area offered to teach me to play piano for free during his free time, but because of my socio/cultural indoctrination, I would not accept. I loved music, but I stopped participating because of the conspicuous presence of homosexuals. I would not be associated with anything they were doing in any way. I understand now that my attitude was more indicative of my own instability than anything else. For example, during the time of my graduation, my father asked me one morning what career choice I would pursue. I told him I wanted to major in music. He asked me if I was crazy and told me I must major in engineering. I explained that I loved music and I had been training with the Detroit Music Settlement School. I told him that this school was regarded as a stepping stone type of training that could launch talented students into a professional life in entertainment and music.

That morning, I remember that I was standing at the foot of my parent's bed. He asked me what had I learned in the training. I remember repeating some ballet terminology before showing him the corresponding ballet movements. When I

41

finished, he looked at me and asked me if I was a sissy. My dream was aborted. Looking back, I now recognize that there was apparently some confusion concerning a possible connection between my musical interests and sexual orientation. I did know that I have never had any thoughts of or intimate desires towards any male. But the fact that I was defenseless against that ignorant attack by the man I called my father, speaks to my vulnerability at the time. Like so many, I was the young victim of my father's ignorance and insensitivity.

Because I expressed an interest in something out of what he considered the norm, I was brutalized by his closed-mindedness. How many young men are lost this way? God only knows. It hurt me deeply when he told me that even though they could comfortably afford it, they would not invest in my education unless I studied engineering, so I conceded. My grades qualified me for a scholarship to Wayne State, but I was so afraid of failing that I didn't apply. Instead, I enrolled at a local junior college into the pre-engineering program. I did miserably, as could be expected, since my heart was not in it. After two months of my first semester in college, I was hired by an automobile manufacturer. But the fifteen credit class load wore me out. Working a midnight shift and carrying a full class load brought me to a probationary status by my second semester. My academic life was doomed. I finally dropped out, but returned a year later.

Clearly, I was just going through the motions. Thug life had become too rooted in me by then. As I mentioned earlier, I had bought a Cadillac in May of 1969. I was nineteen years old. It was powder blue with a white convertible top. I had only paid two car notes before I was fired from my job. I had made an extension cord from scrap and had attempted to take it home. I didn't think it was stealing, but the company did. From the beginning of my appeal process to regain my job, I was a victim of my own drug assisted foolish thinking. As far as I was concerned, they needed me more than I needed a job. Besides, my dope told me that: (1) I had a pocket full of money; (2) I had a Cadillac; (3) I was young; and (4) I was pretty, so what did I need a job for? I never went back to continue fighting for my job. I gave away my job as a millwright apprentice, or more accurately, with my help, I was robbed. Translation - I was a nineteen year old fool.

Before I began shooting dope, I sold it through a Caucasian co-worker. He later became one of the founders of the first methadone clinic in Detroit. He worked for me as I continued to do what I had been trained to do all my life. I was selling pills at the plant. Heroin and weed were being sold for me. My friend's home was about two blocks from the factory. Both of his parents were alcoholics. I had taken over their house. Because of his parents" indebtedness to me, every Friday and Saturday, I hosted after hours parties at their house to reduce their debt. His mother, father and his sister worked for me. I was doing everything that I had been doing all of my life.

I loaned money for 25% interest per week. I followed the tradition that I was raised in. I was taught that everyone was supposed to owe me. I carefully watched to find out what people around me spent their money on so that I could provide it. I didn't care what it was or how much it harmed them. I sold heroin for about a year through my dope runner. Though we were both inspectors, he could move freely throughout the workplace because of his color.

I remember the night I witnessed for the first time someone going through heroin withdrawal. When I usually purchased a quantity of heroin to sell, my worker would portion the powder into capsule form and I would give him a portion for himself. He would sell the "caps" and bring me the money.

On this particular night, something happened with the man that I was supposed to purchase heroin from. My worker got sick and began having symptoms of what I learned later were only the first phases of heroin withdrawal. He kept asking me to go somewhere else to find some dope. I had no knowledge of what withdrawal was all about and I didn't care, but because he kept insisting, I asked him why was he so insistent.

He told me he had a habit and he needed a fix. This meant absolutely nothing to me. I asked him what a habit was and how sick was he going to be. I realized then that I was torturing this man. I asked him more questions and I asked him if he would be willing to beg for that drug. He started crying and said yes. I got angry at him for being so weak.

By the same time one year later, the lack of will power that I saw as weakness in him would have begun the process of enslaving me for the next twenty-seven years. It would cause me to forsake everyone that I ever knew, loved and cared about.

I gave him the money to get what he needed that night and I left. I wouldn't let him sell drugs for me anymore because I was convinced that there was something wrong with him. He told me later that that episode dealing with me was very critical in changing his life. He did what he had to do to kick his drug habit. After kicking his habit he became one of the founders of the first methadone clinic in Detroit.

By the time he was free of active heroin use, I had a heroin habit and was well on my way to the day when I would beg for heroin. One night after I had stopped dealing with him, I noticed a package of heroin on the dresser. I was selling heroin on my own and I was living at my uncle's house. I had mistakenly left some dope sitting out on the dresser uncovered for three days. The word among heroin dealers was that the strength of the dope would fall if left in open air for three days.

That night, I was drinking Boone's farm wine. I'll never forget this night. I rarely smoked weed, but I favored dropping these uppers (pills) regularly. The after effects of taking these pills caused a condition such that when you came down from the high, you would get what we called the "blahs." Your stomach got the butterflies and you'd have headaches the day after.

This Saturday night while I was high on pills, I remembered this new spot I'd heard about called the Drumbeat. I had my Cadillac, a pocket full of money and my hair curled up pretty. Out of curiosity, I sniffed some of my heroin and went to the Drumbeat. I was overcome by the mixture of drugs. The heroin had overpowered the pills. I longed to converse with the women who were trying to talk to me, but I was over-doped. I could barely sit there and nod. I was mad at myself because I couldn't stay awake. Somebody finally did wake me up as the place was closing. I left and went home to sleep.

When I woke up, I didn't have the "blahs" as I expected. I

remember this as clear as if it was today. I was saying to myself that I had finally found a way to enjoy the high of the pills and not have the "blahs." In my mind, I thought now I could just take my pills, sniff some of this stuff and I would be cool the next day. It almost drives me to tears to think about all of the pain and misery that my fateful choice that night caused in my life and in the lives of so many others. That fateful choice has even hurt people I may never know. People have died because of the deadly choice of this poor lost nineteen year old boy/man that night.

That was the day. Within ninety days, I was charged with CCW (Carrying a Concealed Weapon). I had carried a gun for years, but I had never used it. I picked up a woman on the streets one day to take her to make me some money. I took her home where she had a conflict with her ex-boyfriend. I pulled my gun out and put everybody in the house at bay. Somebody that I didn't see that was further back in the house called the cops. I was arrested and jailed. I hid the gun in my armrest, but they found it anyway. I got out on bond. The police couldn't really make a case stick because they wrote the report wrong, so I paid a fine.

In that same ninety day period, I was fired from my job as a millwright apprentice at a major automobile manufacturer. I was charged with another CCW while attempting to rob a prostitute one block from the police station. Talk about stupid! I was trying to get away when the cops saw us in my Cadillac with the top down at 2 a.m. chasing a prostitute on Woodward. We threw the guns away, but I was charged with CCW and sentenced to probation.

After getting me out of jail, as my parents and I left the

county jail, they asked me what was wrong with me. I blamed all my problems on them. I took no responsibility for my own actions. These symptoms marked the beginnings of the darkest period in my life. The onset of the very things that I had vowed as a child not to ever have in my life (i.e. high drama) were now controlling my life. There is a proverb that says that the very things that a man living outside of right standing with God fears, are the things that will happen to him. My life is a witness to the truth of this proverb.

Chapter 4: *Rage*

I was nine or ten years old, and our family was leaving on a day trip during the weekend. Somehow, I did something wrong and my punishment was to be left at home alone. I can clearly remember my anger. I don't remember what I did to cause my punishment, but for some reason, my mother, father and two sisters left me at home. I can still remember the rage inside of me. I found a can opener of the old fashioned design. Its design was that it had a little blade on the end. You could stick it in a can and work your way along the edge of the can to take off the top.

We had this very nice kitchen set; a table with four matching chairs. The chairs had a pleasant, puffy floral design. It looked nice. I remember that I began by stabbing one chair on the upper part of the back. It felt so good that I just kept doing it. Before it was over, I went through all of the chairs in the set. I had methodically destroyed every chair. I mutilated both the seating pads and the back pads with deliberate vengeance. I stabbed each one to pieces. I stabbed them repeatedly.

It felt good even though I knew that I would be beaten when my parents returned home. I knew I was gonna get it; there was no doubt about it. But the certainty of punishment did not faze me at the time. I knew what was coming, but I didn't care. Whatever it was going to be, it was just going to be. I remember my attitude about it so vividly. I knew what was going to happen and I didn't care.

I recall that incident now and other times when I have demonstrated that same anger. It is just by the blessing of God that I no longer have that anger.

It is only the grace and mercy of God that has brought me from being the person that I was. He has removed the anger that was inside that little boy who sought expression through violent outbursts. He is replacing that little boy's anger with God's love. I was that angry child inside crying out, dealing with life through conveniently misguided expressions. The clinical diagnosis would at best be called "dysfunctional" in today's terms, but to only diagnose my condition would not have helped.

The love of God is what that little lost, troubled child needed. I went through some hard times like many others and I dealt with life in a child's way the same as many do. I was only one among many. As I look around today, I see a lot of precious children in grown up bodies that are reacting to life the same as I did. It is God's will that this story will be a witness to some lost soul. Jesus is the answer. Someone may somehow be blessed to vicariously experience my pain and see a different way out instead of repeating the actions that marked my life. Someone may avoid the painful journey of my life and thereby reduce the deep wounds and suffering in their own life. Someone may exercise God's wisdom and not require the Lord to make a personal intervention to heal the wounds of their broken vessel. My life may even represent pain enough for both of us. This is my prayer.

Chapter 5: *I Challenged God*

I was a nineteen year old confused boy wanting to be a man, but not knowing how to be one. I had a job in an auto plant, I had just bought a Cadillac and I thought that I was "all that," as the young folks say today. Looking back, I now have quite a different view of the situation. My life had arrived at a place where I had the audacity to challenge God. I boldly executed a plan that I foolishly thought was a reasonable way to prove to myself the existence of God once and for all.

What I did, in a way, amounted to a prayer. It was more accurately a confounded perversion of a prayer. I said, "If you are God and you are around here somewhere - if you do have power like I was told – I want you to reveal yourself to me and I want you to reveal yourself to me in this way." I told God, "If you can do anything, I challenge you to get me locked up behind bars. Not just that. I challenge you to get me locked up in such a way that no amount of money can get me out." As I write these words, I can't believe that I really did that, but I know that I did.

I was so confident, arrogant and foolish that I actually thought that even God couldn't get me locked up; that even God couldn't fulfill that task. I was certainly convinced that no man could do it. I remember making this challenge.

I only did it once, but the memory is fresh in my mind. It was the summer of 1969. In short term, by the end of August of "69, I was fired from my job as a millwright apprentice. By the fall of "69, I was a penny-ante, hustling bum with a pretty car that my parents were forced to pay for. My meager and truly unpredictable income came from robbery, selling dope, and whatever other menial hustle that I could scrounge up. All this occurred within one year of making the challenge to God. By November of "70, I was arrested and charged with homicide.

As I look back on it now, I can clearly see that I was one very confused, hurting young man. I was a boy seeking manhood in so many wrong ways. I was desperately searching for an acceptable identification: a self-image of some kind for what a man was. I believed that I was without any legitimate role models. I had no confidence that I had anybody around that I could go to with my problems. I believed I was in the world alone. I wanted to be a man, but the criteria that I had as a reference was hodge-podge, at best. My image of a man was solely based upon notions drawn from my environment and my own imagination.

I remember stating on different occasions that this phase of my life was a time for me to make the transition from theory to practice. I believed that the accumulation of my life's experiences should now be transitioned into practice. There was so much pain during these times. Maybe my past will be of benefit to someone else – to some young man going through similar challenges in the process of growing up. I don't have the definitive answer or the definitive procedure for a young man to follow. Most young men don't tend to be as crazy as I was, as extreme as I was, or as confused as I was. My life has occasioned a rather bizarre series of these kinds of episodes.

Maybe the Lord will see fit to use the very bizarreness of my life to instruct someone who reads this book. My life may glaringly display some of the things that are to some measure going on inside other troubled young men. Of course, my real message here is a message of hope. My hope is in Jesus. He was there for me when I needed Him most. He was there for me before I became aware of Him being there. Thankfully, He was there when I finally acknowledged Him. He was there all the time. Someone may be able to avoid some of the misery, pain and suffering that was witnessed in my life and the lives of so many who suffered because of my sin.

This is part of the reason why I am telling this story. I have always been a pretty extreme person, but I had no idea that it would be such an extreme undertaking emotionally to tell this story. It is only because of a conversation between my Beverly and I days ago that even brought my foolish challenge to my remembrance. But, I do remember that episode. It was tragic and traumatic, but it did happen. Because my heart was not right, I did not accept or recognize the apparent consequences of my foolish challenge as they unfolded. He was a God that I did not know. I wasn't ready.

My challenge to God meant nothing to me on the day the judge sentenced me to a mandatory life sentence for first - degree murder. I remember on that day leaning against the bars in a holding cell before I was put back on the jail ward. I was being transported to the cell where they would keep me until it was time to go to Jackson Prison to start serving my life sentence. I had no thought that my foolish challenge had been met and that I had lost. God did not put me in prison but He had allowed me to suffer the consequences of my own foolish behavior. On that particular day, I didn't even remember the challenge. It didn't occur to me until I casually thought about it again sometime later. With sadness, I admit that I learned nothing from the experience until many years later.

As I leaned against the bars in the holding cell that day my nose started bleeding. I remember saying jokingly that it was the first time a man had bloodied my nose without hitting me.

Chapter 6: *Detroit Riot 1967*

This occasion significantly reinforced my attitude about the potential benefits of crime as well as my view of myself in relation to the rest of the world. The riot started on a Sunday morning. It became apparent to my mother and I that no stores were going to be open. That was our rationale and all the excuse we needed. By Sunday night our neighborhood was ablaze. We decided that we needed to make a move. I was seventeen years old and had just graduated from high school. My mother and I have always been very close. We approached my step-father about looting, but as expected, he just wasn't that kind of a crook. He would never participate in such a direct approach to crime. He was a different kind of crook.

My sisters were too young to go looting. I knew everyone in the neighborhood, so I chose a few dependable thieves to go with us. I was the driver. We first canvassed the neighborhood to find a store. We found an A&P. Looters were coming out of the building with frozen parts of animals. Items like quarter portions of cows and halves of hogs: just everything. Because our family was already established as the outlet for stolen items, people soon began bringing us looted merchandise. Now that was right up my father's alley. He wouldn't go out and do anything since people were going to bring the loot to us anyway, and they did.

On the other hand, my mother and I had a peculiarly compatible sense of adventure. We patrolled the neighborhood and picked up a lot of loot. We bought freshly stolen merchandise from people right on the streets.

I would like to emphasize in this segment that the riot of 1967 was not a race riot. The riot in Detroit had nothing to do with race. Some political-type people in the city have misleadingly, if not deceptively, advanced the theory that the riot was related to race. I witnessed no racial conflict violence or vandalism or any racially motivated activities. I looted with white/Caucasian people. In fact, a lot of the looting of stores that occurred was orchestrated by the store owners themselves. I even know a number of local store owners that burned their own stores. (I declined offers to burn businesses.)

The burning of one's own business was used as a means to move on to greener pastures: a well paid ticket out of the hood. From a strictly business standpoint, having no regard for pleasing or even acknowledging God, it is understandable where they were coming from. It was all about money. The riot presented an opportunity for some store owners to make more money. But for our purposes, we were just a bunch of greedy folks in the neighborhood. A lot of the merchandise we took was never used. We simply hoarded whatever we could get.

My family moved from the east side of Detroit three years after the riot, and we still had loot from the riot. We still had canned foods and all kinds of items that we had accumulated during the riot. The camaraderie, the fellowship and the closeness that existed between my mother and I was strengthened during the riot. That ordeal also confirmed the leadership in our house. It went from my mother to me. My father had all but abdicated his authority in the house.

A good example occurred after I started working in the factory in 1967. I decided I would move out to get my own apartment. My mother's objection to that was that if I left, then she would leave too. Her argument was that she felt she had no more usefulness there once I left. I don't know how this will be incorporated into a book, but my mother and I were that close. If the situation had been reversed during that time, I probably would have left my wife and family for her. This is another example of our heart bond.

Sometime not long after I was sentenced to life, I was told that my mother refused to sleep in her own bed. The accommodations of her home were and are not lacking in any area. She not only refused to sleep in her own bed, but she slept on a cot in the basement. Her reasoning was that since I was living in an uncomfortable circumstance in prison, then she wouldn't accept the comforts of her own home until I returned. That exemplifies the character of my mother and how close we were and she did exactly what she said. She did not sleep in her bed for a long time.

Some family members thought she was crazy. I can't speak to that, but I do know that there was no limit to which my mother would not have been willing to go to help me get out. This includes escape. I love her very much. She is facing a challenging time in her life right now, but she will always enjoy my full support as long as life is within me. I just wanted to mention that time of looting with my mother because we laughed more than we stole. We had a really fun time. We were looting up to the time the military was given authorization to shoot. Here we are stealing everything that we could put in our car while the cops and the military people were standing right there looking at us. They were ordered not to lift a hand to stop us. We loved it! They started marching on Tuesday and shooting on Wednesday. We abruptly stopped looting on Wednesday, too. But we had a fun time.

Still, in my way of thinking at the time, the riot just helped my roots go deeper concerning the benefits of crime. I knew beforehand that my mother would loot right with me. Whenever I had any money-making ideas, if it didn't threaten the family directly, my mother's response would be that it was okay – "Let's do it." For example, she gave me the money to buy my first shoebox of marijuana – they called it Acapulco Gold. It was supposedly the strongest weed on the streets.

I sold weed for awhile, but after recognizing it's greater profit margin potential, I switched to heroin and cocaine. I only sold small amounts of cocaine in comparison to heroin because the cocaine market wasn't very good at that time. But heroin was a quite lucrative market. I sometimes made over $1,000 a day selling it.

Chapter 7: *Detroit Homicide*

Since there are so many details that could still prove harmful to other people, I will, therefore, only mention my involvement. I will say, though, that the case for which I was convicted and served time assumes that there were two accomplices. But I have not and will never incriminate anybody. Needless to say, however, this homicide conviction was a monumental landmark in my life. Not only because of the homicide itself, but also because it publicly marked a very tumultuous phase in my life. My prayer is that it will somehow serve to be of some benefit to someone.

Between the first time I sniffed heroin in 1969 and the time I was arrested for first degree murder in 1970, I had transformed from being a hopeful boy seeking to establish a self image as a man, to a little Cadillac driving, slick- head punk. Yes, I am talking about me. But like twenty-one year olds historically, I thought I knew it all. I began my venture into adulthood in the tradition of my parents as a hard worker – just as my mother and father had always been. Following that same tradition, I had a job, but I also had a distorted view of the real purpose for having a job. I thought a job was merely a means to an end. A job was a necessary hazard ; a front. My real money, in my mind, would come from other sources.

In my home, most of our income did come from other sources. I never had a concept of what could be called a socially acceptable job principle. I believed that a job was necessary to supply enough income to hide my crooked money. Why I thought I needed so much money anyway, I will never know. But I did think of a job as a means to an end

58

and I lived like it. For a short period, I made more money in the streets than I did at my job in the automotive industry, but that only lasted for a short season. Now that I think of it, I had a very selfish and immature regard for my family upbringing. I knew that my mother and father would spare no expense to support me in any venture. For example, I got the money for my first shoebox of marijuana from my mother. Selling weed for me was simply following a family tradition.

I started selling weed at home and later attempted to grow it at home. Ironically enough, I attempted to grow it in the same attic where we used to make corn liquor. (I never thought about that before now, but I was actually following precisely the tradition in which I was raised.) I bought a hot light and the right dirt, but I didn't have all the right information to grow it properly.

In other words, again, I was casually repeating and continuing in the tradition that had been passed on to me. But being young and impatient, I became frustrated and abandoned the weed project. Now, I was selling pills (uppers and downers) by the thousands. I was even a loan shark at my job. I had outstanding debts coming to me from people averaging $1,000 a week. (We were only making about a $125 a week at the factory.) Between the loan sharking, the pills, dope selling and my after hour's joint, I was making a lot more in crime than I was making at the plant.

Soon, sin began to take its toll in my life. By the end of 1970, I had been fired from numerous good paying jobs. I finally gave up looking for a job, so I took to the streets full time. I was charged with other felony offences before this homicide. At age nineteen, I pleaded guilty and received probation for armed robbery and carrying a concealed weapon. They charged me with everything connected with the crimes since I was the driver and owner of the car. I was quite a dumb crook, but I thought I was a gangster.

Between August 1969 and November 1970, I decided that most of my associates just had weak hearts. I thought I was tough. I had a gun and access to guns. I had people around me that would do what I wanted them to do without question. I robbed a few folks and cheated a lot of people out of money. I hustled people. I even had a few short term prostitutes. I didn't know until later that if I had a prostitute, she had a prostitute too because I was nothing but a whore myself.

Anyway, my reputation locally was that I was somebody dangerous. I sought to profit from my mediocre reputation through extortion and threatening people to give me their money and dope. At the same time, I deliberately avoided those gangster types I considered the big boys. There were some bad dudes out there that I had only heard about, so I made it my business not to knowingly conflict with or offend certain people.

When this murder charge came up, I was in a dope house along with a person that I had known awhile. We were in a back room shooting our dope. Because his dope was weak, he wanted either the return of his money or some more dope. The dope man originally had conceded that his pack was short, but my associate kept nagging him about it. At some point, one of the dope men said they might not give him anything. The argument progressed to where the dope men said that they had the power to give him nothing and there was nothing he could do about it. Then, here comes Allen. I intervened and told them that they couldn't treat my friend like that. They asked, "Who are you?"

Only one guy in the apartment, the doorman, had a gun. He represented the security of the dope house. He stepped up and told me that I was nothing and that they would take my dope and kick my butt too (he used much more graphic terminology than this). My mindset was that he or anyone else would have only one of three options in dealing with me: he would have the choice to be my friend; he would have the option of getting away from me; or, he would have to kill me and I meant it. He opted to beat my butt, instead.

He came over to me, reached around the guy that I was standing up for and punched me on the side of my head. I got up fully aware that he had the gun and that I didn't have one with me. I ran towards the door. When I got to the door and pulled it, the second chain latch was on it. Something inside of me said that I'd better turn around. I turned around and the guy was bearing down on me preparing to shoot. I started pleading for my life. The man with the gun (the doorman) and the man with the sack (the dope man) started speaking. There were some women in the apartment at the time. The women visibly had an effect on the way that this guy with the gun was trying to portray himself. We were all young and if I were him, I would have probably done the same thing. He wanted to be the macho man; the tough guy.

I knew that I had to plead for my life to keep this guy from shooting me, pistol whipping me and/or violating me anymore. I kept crying and pleading with him for my life. I heard later that they changed their minds about letting me go after I left. I was told that they later tried to find me to trick me back into the dope house. Somehow, they found out about my reputation and that I was serious about my idea of being a gangster.

It was a fatal mistake for them to let me go. I was a young man trying to define my personal identity of my manhood in all the wrong ways. I was in a critical testing phase of my life without knowing it, of course. I needed other people to validate me – I needed other people to confirm a right of passage that should only come from God . I was dangerous.

So, I went outside to the car where I had a sawed off shotgun. I told my boys what had happened and they persuaded me not to go back in there to shoot the guy. They convinced me that I was going straight to jail because everybody would know I did it. They wanted me to let it pass, but, for me, that was out of the question. They even hid a part of my shot gun so that it wouldn't shoot. They took me to my girlfriend's house.

Upon our arrival, my girlfriend started talking to me and I just decided to stay there. All that weekend, I thought about how I would go back to get my revenge. As far as I was concerned, my reputation was at stake. I couldn't let the word get out on the streets that I let a man hit me and live. By Monday, I had convinced my partners that my retaliation would be limited to just robbing the dope house. That would be enough for me. We went round and round about it until they finally accepted going with me.

We went back to the dope house three days later. I went in alone. I sat down, shot my dope and waited. I was never allowed to bring anyone in there with me for obvious reasons. The dope man and the doorman left the dope house to go and get another supply. I followed them outside to get my crew. We waited in the hallway of the building. As we waited, I was seen by people that were later used as witnesses against me at my trial, but my mind was completely blank. I was there to take care of what I considered to be my business. I knew that I was there to kill the guy.

When they did return, I stopped them on the stairway. I stopped the man who usually carried the gun. We searched them, but they didn't have any dope. The supply hadn't arrived yet. The doorman who had hit me showed no fear in the face of death. I didn't like that. He was the only one who actually had showed any heart. I told the guys that were with me that they could leave and I would meet them in the car. They argued that I should not shoot the man, but it was a done deal as far as I was concerned. My one partner went up the steps and I thought that he broke the other guys'' neck. He was supposed to kill him. He was qualified since he had enough knowledge of martial arts and experience to kill him with his hands. But he didn't and why he didn't kill him, I don't know.

However, he did do something to cause him to collapse on the steps. (This man later filed a recanting affidavit, which assisted in my ultimate release five years later.) Yet, at the time, I thought he was dead. I thank God today that I did not on that evening foolishly take another life.

But I did, however, shoot and kill the man who had hit me. We ran from the building. We had been sitting in the lobby waiting for thirty minutes in public view. We then brilliantly rushed out of the building expecting to elude curious eyes. Later on that same night, we robbed another dope house to get some more dope. That same night I asked one of the guys with me, "I wonder if I killed him?"

Here it is I took a sawed off shotgun, aimed it at this man's heart and blew it out and I was actually fearful and wondering if I had killed him. At the same time, I was trying to identify with and project to the world that I was this real gangster. I will forever be grateful for the mercy of God. There is nothing more horrible than standing face-to-face with somebody and killing them.

At the end of the night, I went home as usual to my mother's house and went to bed. May God have mercy on me! The next morning, I got a phone call asking me about leaving town. It was years later that I found out that the caller knew about the homicide and knew that a group of men were looking for me. My next communication was from two homicide officers. They came to my mother's home, and found and confiscated the two disposable parts of the sawed off shotgun. I had shown the gun to one of the guys that frequented the dope house a few months before. He apparently had told the cops this while they were writing their report.

They took me to jail and we then proceeded through the trial process. I was convicted of first degree homicide and was sentenced to what the news commonly calls a life sentence without the possibility of parole. In other words, the parole board could never release me by statute under a first degree murder sentence. The governor would have to commute my sentence before I would be eligible for consideration by the parole board. The only thing that the parole board was authorized to do was to review and submit that review to the governor for possible commutation. That process would not even begin until after the fifteenth year of incarceration.

According to statistics, the average amount of time that people serve for this sentence is twenty-two years. I served four years, 285 days for that charge. I suffered a lot of pain, but I hurt a lot of people. I may never enjoy forgiveness by men for all of the tragedy that I brought to so many people, but I accept that I am forgiven by the word of God and not necessarily by the will of men. This acceptance by God is the only way that I am able to go on.

I know that I am forgiven, but I still sometimes think about how his mother must have suffered as well as countless other people associated with his life. I clearly recognize how the fallout from and the effects of that one shotgun blast has effected and still now affects my family, particularly my biological sons and grandchildren I have never met.

Chapter 8: *First Degree Murder was the Sentence they gave me*

My first prison sentence was life with no possibility of parole for first degree murder. The second sentence was one to fifteen years for unarmed robbery. On the second sentence, I was locked up for four months in a northern Michigan prison camp. Doing time was pretty anticlimactic by the time I served my second sentence. I was a veteran convict. I knew how to live in jail. I didn't, however, learn anything about how to not go back again. I just thought that I had simply been doing crime wrong. I was twenty-one years old the first time and thoroughly convinced that the life that I lived was the life that I was going to continue to live for the rest of my life.

I entered Jackson Prison in June 1971. They called the place quarantine. They processed prisoners there and determined where you would do your time. They would customarily send young offenders under twenty-two years to a place called Ionia. But because I had so much time and even though my age was twenty-one, they gave me an option. Inside the walls of Jackson was considered such a dangerous place that I had to sign a waiver to relieve the corrections department of responsibility for my safety. Without giving it much thought, I decided that I would rather trail blaze or pioneer just one time instead of twice.

I went inside the walls of Jackson Prison on August 5, 1971. When I look back on the whole situation, I recognize now that I was so afraid that I didn't know that I was afraid. (Prisons are populated by men that enter into a massive state of denial as a defense mechanism.) I did, however, have the benefit of a number of loyal comrades that entered the walls at the same time. We were going inside the walls together. Most of them had life and a proven track record of violence. They would support the way I knew I was going to behave.

My first cell block assignment was in one block. The first day I went inside the walls, I went to the desk to register for assignment to a cell. I watched as this inmate opened the cell doors. In his hand was this long piece of steel that looked like a crow bar. I identified him as a highly publicized rapist-murderer. He had the infamous reputation of having committed multiple homicides on women in the Ann Arbor area. I had heard of this guy and he was known for being very dangerous as well as being a pervert. I immediately got a knife. I met a guy that I knew from the neighborhood; we called "Chop –Chop." He was in a feud with some people who were out to get him, although I didn't know about this at the time.

On the sixth day that I was inside the walls, as chop-chop and I entered our cell block after breakfast, this guy came up behind us and hit me in the head with a pipe. He then hit Chop-Chop a number of times also before running off. Over the next couple of weeks, there were a number of assaults that took place. I couldn't retaliate immediately because the authorities knew the identity of our assailant. If I retaliated too soon, they would come straight to me. We also couldn't press charges because that wasn't the way that we dealt with things. Later on, some of my friends cut up the guy that had hit me. They also beat Chop-Chop with a pipe for not telling me about his situation. This was my initial introduction inside the walls.

So, I went on through the procedures. They gave me a job working in the shoe factory after I had gone through processing. They tried to find something for me to do since I was going to be there a very long time. I worked in the shoe factory for two weeks before they called me in and told me that I couldn't work there anymore. They said that for the two weeks that I worked there, they had lost the entire stock of shoes. They next sent me to work in the cleaners.

In the cleaners, I developed a relationship with a man they called "Red Dog." He was a feared young man. He was one of a crew along with two others. We grew very close during those years in Jackson. In the news, Gunsby, a.k.a. "Red Dog," and his co-defendants were called the "vigilantes of the underworld." Red Dog and I started taking over the laundry. The homosexuals working in the laundry sold laundry services by cleaning and pressing prisoner's uniforms. We started having them work for us until violent conflicts associated with the laundry business began to increase. They knew that Gunsby, Sunny Man and I were involved, so they put us out of the laundry.

About this time, I inquired about the night school college program. Entering the program allowed me total exemption from prison work details. In 1972, I started classes at the branch of Jackson Community College located inside the walls at Jackson Prison. At this point, I was not really involved in any criminal activities. I was just wild and mainly trying to adjust to how I was going to deal with this life sentence. I had no concrete plan or expectations. It didn't make any difference to me if I was going to break out or if I would get out through the courts. I knew that my family would support me financially if and when a way was found.

They had my back. In fact, my mother visited me on every visiting day.

This period lasting from the time I was first arrested in November 1970 to the time that I was released on an appeal bond in July 1975 was almost five years. Jackson was, in most ways, a negative learning experience. I learned how to do crime right, if there is any such term. I became rooted in the execution of crime from the perspective of men that had been doing crime their entire life. In short, it was a crime school. It was not only a training camp for learning how to execute crime, but also for indoctrination in the mindset to embrace crime as a lifestyle. It was accepted by my associates and I as simply a career choice.

An example of this distorted idea of respect would be when someone felt they had been publicly disrespected. A certain offended person was robbed while conducting the business of selling weed. Though he was not assaulted during the robbery, the robbers bragged about their conquest around the yard. One night one of the robbers was set up. Visiting hours were until 9 p.m. and the visiting length allowed was usually two hours. Sometimes, a prisoner was privileged to receive a visitor that had arrived late. Since they sometimes couldn't enter the visiting room due to overcrowding, they would be allowed at least a few minutes.

The block clerk received a call and the information was given to the guard. The prisoner dressed for his visit, but on the way to the visiting area, he was ambushed. His eye was cut out and he was disemboweled. He was able to walk to the hospital with his guts in his hands. He survived somehow, though the intent was clearly to kill him and he knew it. With respect restored, the matter was settled.

These are the kinds of things that I was involved in and took pride in at the time. This is the lifestyle that I adapted to and identified with while I was in prison. And this lifestyle – my lifestyle - in prison continued to produce predictable consequences.

There arose an occasion when I believed that I had lost pictures of a woman that I was seeing prior to my incarceration. I believed that they were just lost until I discovered that somebody had stolen them, reproduced them and was selling them to men on the yard. Following this discovery, I found the thief. I initially told the guy that he had until the end of the day to recover every copy he ever had made. I explained to him that it wasn't about the girl and it wasn't about the pictures. It was about the fact that he had taken something from me. I couldn't allow the word to get out that things could be taken from me. By mid-day, I decided not to wait until the end of the day. I found the guy and I beat him in the head with a pipe. He was taken to the hospital , I was put in solitary confinement for a week and scheduled to be transferred to another prison for security purposes.

Because I was locked up the pressure on him from the guys that I knew out on the yard became intense. After a few days he volunteered that he was the cause of our conflict and he should be the one locked up instead of me. He was transferred to another prison in northern Michigan. I was told that they knew what really happened, but with his confession they had no choice but to let me out. This was characteristic of my prison life.
On another occasion, I suffered a near death experience. I was

poisoned. Someone obtained some form of poison and people were dying like flies. Apparently, they were putting the poison into potato chips and different snack foods during our time at the movies. At the end of every movie certain people just didn't get up. I never found out who or exactly how they got me.

I was living in an honor block at that time. Our cell doors were always opened and usually unattended. One day, I started throwing up everything. I was vomiting continuously. I had a lot of canned foods that my family had sent me along with other items including a lot of fruit cocktail .I kept drinking this fruit cocktail for three or four days.

As soon as anything hit my stomach It would always come back up. I didn't know what was wrong.

By the fourth day, the guys that knew me said I looked real bad. I had lost a lot of weight and they believed I needed to go to the hospital. I had been poisoned and I was near collapsing. So now I had been poisoned along with being beat in the head. What a life I had made for myself in prison.

There were also other attempts to set me up to kill me. There were even times when I believe I was set up to be raped. Based on what I have seen, in the eyes of a sex starved prisoner, I might have been viewed as an attractive candidate. I started shaving two years after I was inside the walls. I weighed about 170 pounds and I was young. I might have appeared to be a likely prospect subject to a change of heart or a change of mind under pressure. Some prisoners prided themselves in setting up and seducing certain weaker prisoners. Other guys they just gang raped. Thank God it never happened to me.

I remember another time at the end of my second year after classes had begun. I was locking in 4 Block next to 5 Block, which was the disciplinary block. I was in the block for the messed up guys. An incident occurred where a gun tower guard had asked to shake me down. I didn't want him to shake me down because I was carrying a blackjack. It was made from two bars of soap tied together with broken pieces of a razor blade embedded in the soap. The soap was completely covered with embedded razor blade pieces inside of a sock. Then, there was a string going from the soap to the inside of the sock and was finally connected to a knot in the sock.

I only carried a knife when I was definitely going to do something, but I carried this weapon on a regular basis and I got away with this for a long time. In the absence of close examination, it looked like I just had a sock in my pocket. The gun tower guard that stopped me thoroughly examined me. They could have charged me with carrying a concealed weapon. It didn't matter anyway since I had life already, but I was still put in the hole.

The hole was a segregated disciplinary cell block. I stayed in there for almost a year. It was during that experience that I was forced to learn how to live with myself. I learned to live alone in an 8 x 10 concrete room in my underwear with only a toilet. My meals were given to me through a little hole . If I caused any more problems, they would put me in a soundproof cell in total darkness. They were only allowed to keep a man in the slammer for twenty-four hours maximum. A lot of guys lost it in the slammer and never recovered. They would go from the slammer directly to the psych ward. Thank

God I never had to go to the slammer.

On one occasion while in maximum security, I began to identify with a very crazy tradition. Prisoners would sometimes want to be moved to a different cell just to break the monotony. They would throw a mixture of feces and urine in the passing guard's face. The guard would then get the goon squad who would forcibly take the prisoner to the slammer and after twenty four hours, to a new cell. Somehow, it got around to being my turn to do it, but God was on my side. I didn't throw the liquefied waste on the guard. Instead, I verbally challenged the guard sufficient enough for him to assure me angrily that he would be right back with the goon squad.

My uniform in the hole was a pair of elastic-waist pants and a pullover top. The tradition was to tie your head up with the pants and take off the top. Upon the goon squad's return, I would fight and get as many blows in as I could until I was unconscious. They would also bring a spray to assist in disabling the prisoners. When the guard left, I put on my war clothes and prepared for my beating. When I look back at it now, it is clear that I was both bored and insane. We looked at it as being tough and I desired to be thought of in that way. I didn't, however, desire it bad enough to challenge the guard with that disgusting mix. But for some reason, that guard never came back and I don't know if I ever saw him again.

After being in the hole for about a year, prior to my release from segregation, I was moved from 5 West to a lower level maximum security unit called 5 East. In 5 East, I could leave my cell to receive meals. Once a week, I could go outside to a restricted area and get some fresh air. One of the guys that I came across in there was an accomplice to a homicide. He was serving a sentence in Ionia, but had been transferred to Jackson. He was put in a cell right next to me. I immediately became paranoid. I thought they were setting me up. I thought they were using this guy to put the final nail in my coffin. They knew that I had accomplices. They had even offered me the option to tell in exchange for leniency.

So when I saw him, I thought that he had made a deal to implicate me in other crimes and help them lock me down for good. I was very leery of him.

Consistent with his character, he had been put out of Ionia Reformatory for starting a riot. During that same time, I met another man who became a very loyal friend. Having only a two to four year sentence, he was one of the few people I associated with who had such a small amount of time to serve. Most of the people that I dealt with were lifers or people I had known from the streets. But we developed a close relationship. By the time I was released from the detention block, both of these guys were on the yard inside Jackson. They had different violations of prison rules that required them to stay inside the walls with me. I connected them with the guys that I had associations with and they became loyal soldiers.

When I got out of the hole, my reputation on the yard had escalated to the point where the leader of the largest gang sent a message asking me to join in with him. He acknowledged me as being a leader of a group that had earned respect inside the walls. I knew then that I was in.

We didn't make a lot money doing anything. There were a lot

of splinter groups. We stood primarily to represent sure violence as our single defense. People in our "family" pretty much did what they wanted to, but everyone knew that if you went against anyone in our group, then you had to be ready to defend yourself against the whole group.

We stood about seventy-five people strong and we were as large as any group of violent, young, strong, stupid men in prison. That is the best way that I can describe us. That is how we survived. It is only now that I can look back on it and see that we were brought together by fear.

At any rate, by the time I left Jackson in 1975, I had calmed down in the sense that I was not so prone to executing violence spontaneously and indiscriminately. I started to learn how to think about things somewhat, but violence was still a high priority option for me. I had been brought up in this culture. Prison had only aggravated and accelerated the immediate need for survival in me. By the time I left prison in 1975, I believed I was confirmed as a certified gangster. I knew and was known by every publicly known crook in and around Detroit. The sad product of this surely contributed to my further demise. This process continued from 1975 to when I hit rock bottom in 1995. By 1995, I was a destitute and homeless dope fiend.

A lot of those prolonged years were innocently enabled by my family. (I am sure they regarded their support as their way of showing love for me.) Most of my financial support was via my own working efforts. For a long while I was still able to keep up the façade of social acceptability by earning my own money.

For many years, I was blessed to have a job through which I

could make a substantial amount of money. I had access to the criminal world involving numerous aspects of different criminal activities as well. I could often go to these people and get what we called consignments. I could get drugs to sell with no up front money. I could also get consignments for other criminal enterprises. There came a time where I made it known that I was available for contracts on people's lives for a price. It is not like I had any notions of being some big shot hit man or anything; I was not. I was just willing to do almost anything for money and / or dope.

These activities only served as a means of maintenance for my dope use. I spent a lot of time away from my family. I am only now beginning to know my sons. I can't know what good telling this story will do, but this was what my prison life was like. These pages contain revelations that I am only now coming to understand. There developed in me a hardness; a hard core grew around my heart during this period. Some things I would have considered consciously before prison, I could now execute with total insensitivity (i.e., without a second thought). I knew by the time that I was released that I was capable of doing anything to anybody at any given time and feel absolutely nothing. I had no remorse. I was virtually psychopathic.

A close associate of mine was part of a riot that went on one night in 4 Block. The riot began with certain prisoners trying to assault a man for sex. The violence escalated to the point where the guards had to call on the gun tower sharpshooters to restore order. In the confusion, one officer was running down the gallery. This guy I know was approaching the guard to stab him, but someone attacked the attacker before he could get to the officer. The officer was pushed into one of the cells accidentally and somehow became locked in the cell. When the guards finally regained control of the situation, everyone involved was put in solitary confinement.

The would-be attacker was mistakenly thought to have saved the officer's life. The officer never realized that this man had actually planned to stab him. This man was mistakenly released from the hole though he was a co-conspirator in starting the riot.

The entire group was quite frankly a bunch of predatory rapist - murderers. They extorted money from prisoners and a few of them were known sex predators. The member of the group that I knew was released by virtue of the officer's statement. He soon came to me with a scheme by which he might get special parole consideration for saving the life of a guard. Saving the officer's life alone wouldn't make him eligible for this type of special parole because of his murder conviction. So the plot was for this man to be assaulted and stabbed in his cell. He would say that the guys on the yard were going to kill him because he was now thought of as a snitch for helping the officer.

One morning, I went to his cell and I stabbed him eight times. I remember this incident because I remember sticking him as he sat on the bed bleeding. The wounds weren't very deep, but I can still remember standing there feeling nothing as I stabbed him. I remembered how I used to not like to fight as a child and how I didn't like to hurt people. How, during a fight, I would usually cry because I knew that I was hurting someone. That was a measure of a gift that God had given me, but no one was around to help me learn how to develop that gift to the glory of God.

I am pretty much back to my childhood way now. When I go to homeless shelters to talk to people, a lot of times I can't talk to them because I am too overwhelmed with tears. I can actually feel the pain of the people sitting there in those chairs coupled with the memories of my own miserable life revisited. On other occasions, while ministering or just having a conversation with someone, I begin to feel their pain. I deliberately stay away from people a lot because if I get too close, I will feel their pain and I begin hurting for them. But, that day, as I was sticking him, I didn't feel anything. It just felt juicy like I was sticking a knife in a piece of meat and not a person. There was no sense that this was a living human being that I was sticking.

This is but one personal example that I can tell you about. To expand on that thought in consideration of the procession of like-minded convicts being released from prisons daily should be frightening. There is a very real potential danger in sending young people to prison and allowing them to freely intermingle with experienced convicts. I realize now that I was innocently and consentingly exposed to a multitude of deadly demonic forces. When my trial judge was trying to restore my life sentence during my appeal process, he sent a memo to the judge that my case had been transferred to. He stated that I should never be allowed to be around civilized people again. This was a private memo that I received because of a relationship that I had with a police officer who was assigned to the court where my case was being heard.

This officer friend became privy to this memo. The information transferred to me was obviously unsettling as I was awaiting sentencing for second-degree murder. A cash deal had been made for my release, but even so, I was still looking at what this judge who was about to sentence me had received from my trial judge.

The worst part about all of this is that at that time, the judge was right in his recommendation. The second judge did, however, go on to do what he was paid to do. I am convinced that God was in charge of the whole affair. It was not about money or the law. God had mercy on me and gave me the chance to come back and glorify him through the misery and horror of my past. He has blessed me way more than I deserve. I will forever give him all of the honor, the glory and all the praise. I owe it to Him to offer my life as a living testimony of gratitude for what He has done for me. What a meager token of appreciation I can offer for this enormous debt I can never repay.

Chapter 9: *Going Back*

On two very memorable occasions, I believe I was touched by the power of God. During these short intervals, I believed I could really see a way out of the prison of my dope life. These times I call "going back."

In 1980, I was married to the mother of my two sons. We lived in an apartment in Highland Park and we had been married three years. She had been baptized in the Holy Spirit a number of years before. Ironically enough, she was ministered to by the woman who is now my wife, Beverly. On this particular day, July 23, 1980, my wife asked me to take her to church. I was living a double life (i.e., part time family man and husband and part time street thug). I was a laid off millwright apprentice. Money was even shorter than usual at our house. In fact, I had adapted to the lifestyle of not having enough quite well.

I clearly remember that on that day I was irritable, but I wasn't suffering withdrawal symptoms. I was more addicted to the lifestyle of the street drama than I was physically in bondage to the drugs, so I drove her to the church. My initial plan was to drop her off, but she asked me to wait for her. As I was waiting in the hallway, a lady asked me to come in and sit down; I did. The lady then told me that she was going to pray. She asked me to pray with her. I said, "Why not." I don't know, I can't really say whether or not this scene at least in part was set up by my son's mother. But I do believe that it was set up by God.

By the time I left that room, I had experienced speaking in

tongues and I had confessed to having the Holy Ghost. I felt clean. I felt as if I had been dipped in a pool that had some kind of liquid in it that was made of a special cleanser. I didn't understand at the time that the cleanser I felt was the blood of Jesus. I felt as if I had been cleaned from the inside; as if I wasn't dirty anymore. I was forgiven.

I started going to church every day. Within weeks, I was asked to appear on the church's television broadcast. I gave my testimony. A pattern soon developed. I was asked to participate in the broadcast every week. Within four months, I convinced myself that I could minister to the people down on the street corners where I used to hang out.

During this time, there was a shortage of heroin on the streets. The drug addicts that I was associated with were substituting a combination of synthetic drugs that we called "T's" and "blues" for heroin; it was a concoction consisting of the pharmaceutical drugs pyrabenzamine hydrochloride and talwin. We would crush these pills and dissolve them in lukewarm water. The solution that resulted would be drawn into a needle and shot.

By Christmas, I was back on the corner. Some Monday evenings I can remember the abomination of sitting in the dope house getting high while watching reruns of myself on TV. I would narrate the pre-recorded broadcast to the other addicts in the dope house. I was so deceived that I believed I was actually ministering to the people getting high with me; I actually thought I had a testimony. I believed that my life was a witness to the power of God.

My behavior was shameful. If it were not for my hope that by telling this episode somebody may avoid a lot of wasted time, hurt and pain, I would never tell anybody this. It is very shameful. My heart's desire is that the Lord might be glorified even through my foolishness. I did do this and by the end of 1980, at thirty years of age, I was fully back out on the streets. My son's mother was still going to church and trying her best to hold onto whatever semblance of a family she could. It's shameful what she had to go through because of me.

I went back to my old world. If there was someone around me close enough to speak to me about the need of being rooted – the need to be still and becoming really solidly changed by the power of God – I didn't hear them. For awhile, I blamed my falling away on everyone else – I was a baby in the Lord and the church just didn't do their job. They didn't minister to me and didn't baby me. Actually, I see now that my heart just was not right. I was not ready yet. I was a classic example of one of those seeds that fell among thorns. I sought out the very environment from which I came. I enabled the deeply rooted sinners, of which I had been chief, to just smother the very beginnings of what the Lord wanted to do in my life. I went back out there and by November 1980, I was headed for prison again.

I committed an unarmed robbery on the street corner where I hung out. A woman wanted to buy some dope. I strong armed her; took her money and food stamps and walked away. What a big shot gangster fool I was. She called the cops and before that day was over, I was locked up for unarmed robbery. I was in the county jail for about three months. The bishop of the church got me out of jail on bond pending trial. I went on the broadcast that same evening, but I conveniently didn't talk during the broadcast about the fact that I was facing new charges.

I eventually pleaded guilty to unarmed robbery. I was sentenced to one to fifteen years and sent back to prison. For four months, I remained at a place called Camp Pellston in the northern part of Michigan's lower peninsula. I learned nothing from my sentence except how to commit crimes with more confidence. I was released in the spring of 1981. I was once again a full fledged sinner and a dope fiend. I joined the methadone clinic again. My life became business as usual. All I had to figure out was how to get me some dope every day. I totally turned my back on my brief taste of freedom.

During those short months of temporary release, I communicated with only a few believers. I had felt a cleanness, a sense of power in the beginning. Thinking back on it now, I was like a kid in a candy shop: a typical baby Christian. I could actually sense that something was available to me that I can only identify as power, but I didn't know what to do with it. I didn't know who to ask about it and I was quite impatient. I didn't ask anybody about it and that proved to my own undoing. I went back. I returned to my own vomit just like scripture says a fool will do.

Another incident occurred in 1990. In January 1989, I suffered multiple injuries from a car accident. They say that I died on the operating table a couple of times. Following those injuries, I was put on social security disability and I received workers compensation. For over two years, I received $4,000 a month, tax free. Usually, by the end of each month, I owed people money for outstanding dope bills. I had developed a $200 a day heroin habit.

At the end of a period ending in the first part of 1992, I began receiving a monthly disability check for $600. One day while in the area where I usually bought my dope, I ended up staying the night in the Cass Corridor. I had doped, drank and drugged until I was penniless. I was forced to spend the night at the NSO Homeless Shelter. I had a house on the other end of town, but I couldn't get there because I didn't have any money. One of my injuries from the car accident was to my leg, so I couldn't do a lot of walking. That night, I slept in a chair at the homeless shelter. The next day, a church group came to the shelter to take people to another shelter.

During this time, there arose a politically inspired urgency around the country concerning the problem of homelessness. A number of people in Detroit exploited the situation by setting up homeless shelters anywhere that they could find a place to put a bed. These "shelters" included churches and/or anywhere else they could find a building to rent or buy.

So that day, I joined a group of men that were transported to a shelter in Inkster, Michigan. It was a homeless shelter owned by the sister of a man that I would come to know later. I stayed the night there. My reasons for staying were that they promised to give us some food, let us take a shower and give us a place to sleep for the night. It all sounded good to me, so I stayed. My plan was to get back to Detroit and go back home to continue my dope hunting lifestyle, but they told us that we had to go to a church service. They took us to a church service that was associated with the ministry that ran the homeless shelter. The owner of that shelter was the sister of the pastor of the church. This incident marked my initial acquaintance with Sister and Pastor Jackson. Something happened to me the first day that I went to their service. I decided, for reasons I didn't understand at the time, to stay another day. I wanted to go back to that church.

The next day, the pastor's wife gave the alter call invitation at the end of the service. I accepted the invitation and I joined. Something lit up inside of me and I knew it. It was like a fire had been rekindled deep inside of me. I felt that power again. I remembered that same feeling of power that I had felt almost ten years before when I first received the baptism of the Holy Ghost. Ten years had gone by since that day at Solomon's Temple, but I hadn't forgotten that feeling of empowerment. I was drawn to this ministry.

Leaving the shelter in Inkster and my house in Detroit, I joined the ministry in Monroe, Michigan. While living there, I began to move up in their ministry. The pastor began to allow me minimal responsibilities in his ministry. The empowerment of God - the infusion of His power - was upon me and I knew it. I could feel it, but again, I didn't know how to handle it. Within six months, I had re-established a relationship with my ex-wife. I ended up moving away from Monroe to live with her again. This was my second wife. We were living in sin again trying to make things work for us our own way. And Beneath all of these other challenges, I still had a drug problem that I was not delivered from yet.

Her seductive deception coupled with my fleshly desires proved to be sufficient stumbling blocks for me. By the end of 1991, I was locked up again. I was arrested for outstanding traffic tickets. I was sentenced to forty days. While there, my now ex-wife informed me that she didn't want to pursue our relationship any longer. Upon my release from jail I went back to my mother's home.

As I look at my own writing about "going back," I am forced to consider how I was tricked; how I was so weak and how I felt so isolated. All these same factors contributed to my falling away again. I hear people say "I found Jesus," but I say, "I didn't find Jesus. He wasn't lost. I was the one lost."

I believe that my journey can best be expressed by saying that I tripped and fell and stumbled my way into the open arms of Jesus. His throne of grace and mercy was there for me when I needed it in spite of myself. I look back sometimes at these short periods when I can remember having the fire of God bubbling inside of me.

I think about my potentially deadly condition of not being teachable or open to instruction. I look at the despair of not having the confidence that there was anybody or somewhere that I could go to get the kind of help I needed. I knew that I had a taste of something that was precious, but I didn't know how to keep it or develop it. I didn't know how to seek out anyone or any place that could assist me in my desire to know Him. As I think back now, I ask myself these questions: "Why didn't I call on the Lord and ask Him for His help? Why didn't I petition Him with an outcry from my heart like I did that day in that vacant building? Why didn't I ask Him to deliver me?"

I don't know. All I know is that this is what happened to me. The Lord has mercifully permitted me to talk about it. May God's will and purpose be fulfilled by these words serving to benefit somebody, somewhere, to lessen the pain or maybe even avoid some of the stumbling blocks that I fell victim to.

Chapter 10: *Role Models*

There were a few people I admired and deliberately sought to mimic what I imagined to be enviable aspects of their character. In my quest for a sense of self-identity, I naturally looked first to those in my immediate environment.

One very prominent person in this category is a man named Arnold C. I don't know if Arnold is still alive, but he was the husband of one of my Uncle Jimmy's stepdaughters. Uncle Jimmy and Kate lived in Chester, Pennsylvania. Jimmy was my mother's oldest brother. My mother looked up to Jimmy. Kate had three daughters by a previous marriage and Gloria was one of her daughters. Gloria married a man named Arnold C. Among black folks in the neighborhood, Arnold was regarded as a gangster and one to be respected. To my knowledge, he earned his respect by being a good fighter and someone who demanded respect on the streets. He became a real gangster in his later years.

I met him as a teenager. I admired the way he conducted himself and the way he dressed, but most of all, the way he was respected. I recall one visit in particular during the Christmas season. Aunt Kate had a nephew my age whose name was Tony. He and I liked to party and dance like most kids our age. I remember one night as we were leaving to attend a party. Arnold told me something that I guess Tony must have already known. Arnold told me that if I ever got into any conflict around Chester, I only needed to mention his name and everything would be all right. I didn't think anything more about it. I didn't consider myself a tough guy by any means. I knew I dressed well and my parents always saw to it that I had a few dollars in my pocket. I wasn't afraid to fight; I could handle myself.

We went to the party and somebody did approach me. It was some guy who was jealous about the attention I was getting from a local girl. He started making moves and asking the kinds of questions designed to provoke an argument. I could see that it wasn't going to be a fair fight between just him and I. He had some buddies there and I was going to be outnumbered. I knew Tony would not fight. I was going to be taken advantage of and either hurt, cut or worse. But before it could escalate to that, I remembered what Arnold had told me. At the mention of Arnold's name, the guy started apologizing to me. Not only did he apologize, he began acting friendly towards me and before it was over, he was even introducing me to girls at the party.

When I saw that all this was just at the mention of Arnold C's name, it was very impressive to me as a young fellow. I took that to heart. I wanted people to respect me like that. I wanted to be looked at that way. Arnold C was a gentleman, superficially. He had the reputation of being somebody who would only hurt you if he had to. He was feared by people and I liked that. He was one of my role models.

Another role model to me was a man named Casey. He was a contemporary of my father. They worked together at a menial job in a barrel reconditioning factory. What I learned about Casey at a very early age was that Casey had served time in prison; he had committed at least one homicide. Among his peers, he was feared and respected. Casey was considered a gangster even though he worked every day. He carried himself in a way that gained the respect among his peers. He was a man to be feared on the basis of his unpredictability. People believed he might do anything to you at any time. He wore his hat in the opposite way from the traditional Ace–Deuce. (The traditional style was rolled up in the back and crimped down in the front a bit. The style mimicked the way the gangsters on TV wore their hats.) Casey wore his hat rolled up in the front, tipped to the side and crimped down in the back. He took that look from the style worn by Al Capone.

When I wore hats as a young man, I wore mine like Casey and Al Capone. I identified with the fear that Casey had among his peers. I identified with the fact that he was feared as one willing to go farther than anyone else in the execution of violence. He would kill you. He was also a cheater at gambling and everybody knew it. He was known to carry a gun and was willing to use guns and knives.

I identified with those kinds of images, so I understand when I see young men looking up to certain guys like I did Casey . They don't know the real fear and misery that often motivates the people they look up to. I see them identifying with the superficial images of these guys just as I did without knowing their real lifestyle. Oftentimes their real lives drastically contradict what their 'fronts' depict , nor do their public image reflect their real character. Some of these role models didn't even choose their public image. For many of them, it was something that just happened to them and they just didn't know how to shake it. Many of them just didn't have what it took to go on and develop what was really deep in their heart. Most of these people never found out who they could have become. Hopefully, my past misery may prove to be a message of hope to some young and/or not so young person trapped where I have been.

My next role model was my uncle Matthew. Matthew was a man that was married to my mother's sister. Toy came to Detroit as a country girl from Alabama and lived with her big sister, my mother. As a very young country girl in the city, she met Matthew and was overwhelmed with love at first bite. He swept her off her little country feet. She left my mother's house to marry him. But Matthew had a reputation as a womanizer. He drank a lot, drank hard and he played hard. He liked to fight and he was good at. He was feared and it was known that Matthew would cut you. He was kind of crazy, actually. He would deliberately go farther than anyone else. He was very jealous hearted, too. He was very vindictive and quite physically imposing and he knew it. He would leverage his propensity for threatened violence against his peers. They shied away from him because he was dangerously unpredictable when drinking and he drank all the time.

The first memorable impression I have of him is when he bought me a Wild Bill Hitchcock gun set. It was a holster and had two toy pistols. I was seven years old. I remember the conflict between my parents and Matthew because they told him not to buy the gun set for me, but my aunt Toy was able to use my mother's love for her younger sister to get my parents to accept the gift for me. I loved that pistol set. I can still see it in my mind's eye. I treasured it. My uncle Matthew had a special place in my heart because of that gun set. Added to that was the kind of respect and fear other people had of him. Their fear of him reinforced my esteem for him.

Prior to my incarceration in 1970, I sometimes hung out with Matthew. I was nineteen years old at the time. He would start fist fights. By this time I was carrying a gun every day. I would always back him up. Though I never had to shoot anybody, I would have if needed. On occasion, I have had to rescue him from groups of people at gun point. Yet, as I became more serious with guns and other criminal activity, his antics became foolishness to me. He was causing me to get into situations that would require unwanted police attention. I really didn't have time to be involved in his foolishness anymore. I was getting serious about what I was doing on the streets. He had no monetary objective or motives to his actions. He was into drinking and having fun womanizing. I wasn't into that. I thought that I was a real gangster and I thought that I had graduated into bigger stuff. I stopped hanging out with him. His lifestyle eventually killed him via cirrhosis of the liver. He died just after I went to Jackson.

In fact, soon after I reached Jackson, I received word that Matthew was told by his doctors that he was going to die within months. They say he made the preparations for his burial on his death bed. I was told that he asked his wife to tell me to take care of his four daughters just before he passed away. I sent word to him that I would do as he asked. His oldest daughter Tammy and I corresponded throughout my incarceration. We have a special relationship even today. We have sometimes held back tears when we saw each other because of the close bond that existed between her father and I.

Above all else, my first role models are my mother and father. I especially identified with the period of our relationship when I was a young adult. This period was before I was using any drugs between the ages of seventeen and nineteen. I didn't like marijuana because it made me feel weak and vulnerable. I am sure that my emotional and mental state at that time had a lot to do with that as well. But, I did like to hang out with my parents.

They maintained their business through numbers, after hour joints, selling liquor and selling all kinds of merchandise.

Again, by age nineteen, I had an after hour joint. I had people selling dope for me. I had prostitutes. I was living the image and I thought that I was "all that." I thought that I was on my way to becoming a big time gangster in Detroit. I can recall going to after hour joints with people that were coordinated in our network of after hour joints around town. Many of these people knew us. My mother, my father and I became well known in our little area. My parents and I would spend hundreds of dollars at these spots. We called it giving a fellow hustler a play. We would spend money at their affairs and they would do likewise when we had something going on. At that time, spending a few hundred dollars in one night was considered a lot. They gave us respect because we had money, we looked the role and we weren't stingy. They treated us like we were special.

I also liked being with my mother; we think a lot alike. My mother and I were so close that on some occasions, we could talk without using words. We could sometimes communicate by looks alone. My father was a good gambler. He was good at playing cards. He knew how to cheat and a lot of people were afraid to play him. He had respect and he liked that.

We had a good time just being together. They were my heroes. I modeled a lot of my ways from their examples that are yet to be worked out of me. They were a vital part of what shaped the way I saw myself even during the down days of my drug addiction. My mother and father were and are my heroes in more ways than I could ever explain. There was never a lot of outward show of affection in our home, but every benefit of street knowledge that they had, they made sure that I was the first in line to receive it.

I was always the first recipient of every detail of any knowledge related to how to get paid. My mother gave me the full benefit of her life's experience in how to handle people. I thank God today that the Lord chose to give me an undeserved opportunity to use these skills to help others.

I was taught everything I learned for the single purpose of taking advantage of people. I was taught that everything beneficial that I could develop was to be used against people, to profiteer off of them; to only benefit myself and those close to me. There was no other use for my gifts and talents. I know now that we had it all wrong. The word of God states that "to whom much is given much is required." Any God given gifts that I have are to be developed by God to be used to His glory alone. He is turning many things around in my life and throwing a lot of things out of my life. He is a great and merciful God, and I thank him for having mercy on me.

Joe K. was a very special role model. Strong emotions accompany what he meant in my life. I met Joe K. while I was in Jackson doing life. He was doing life, too. I met him in 1972. I was put in the high security cell block because they said I was "incorrigible." Joe had been incarcerated since 1958. He was convicted of being involved in a kidnap/murder involving one of the heirs of a very wealthy and prominent family in Detroit. Every time he went to a parole hearing, the family lawyers of the deceased would come to oppose his release. His co-defendants had all pleaded guilty and been released, but he would not admit his guilt.

He was some kind of guy. He was an ex-marine: hardcore to the core. He knew my father from the bootleg days on the east side of Detroit. He took me under his wing. I walked the yard in Jackson Prison daily with Joe from 1972 until I left in 1975. He was in his late forties and was well respected and feared. He was not actively involved in any prison criminal activity; he said he was getting too old for that, but he still liked to gamble.

He was like a retired gangster, like a godfather. Everybody knew of his highly publicized case. Everybody knew who he was and they respected him. I gained a lot of respect through Joe. Prisoners assumed certain things about me because of my relationship with him. They knew I wasn't faking the gangster role because of my association with Joe. Joe K. impressed me by being a very strong willed person. He was a stubborn person. He was so stubborn that he stayed beyond the time he should've been in prison because he refused to openly admit to his guilt.

He recognized my desire to be a pseudo intellectual and my voracious appetite for books and learning so he exposed me to everything he knew. He started me reading the Bible on a regular basis. He told me that he wanted me to read the book as I would any other book (i.e., like a novel). So, I began reading the Bible on my own in 1972. It is quite a different book now.

Today, I can only remember those years of bible reading as so many stories. Today, I feed on it as the word of God because of the literal food that it is proving to be to my spiritual life. It is now an instruction manual and much more. I study the same scriptures from a much different perspective these days. I see things that otherwise I would never have noticed because of the way my heart and mind are being transformed.

Joe also introduced me to Hitler's autobiography. I became fascinated by the life of Hitler. I did extensive research on Hitler and tried to get inside of his head. Some things that I discovered in my studies now I wish that I didn't know about Hitler or myself. I was also led in the course of my research to embark on the study of a subject called "nihilism." It is the philosophy of nothingness. I learned from Joe K. to develop the attitude of murder. Before meeting Joe, I had more than enough anger and hatred inside of me to be receptive to his instruction. Of course, I did not know this about myself until much later. But I had internalized a temperament by the time I left Jackson such that I could walk up to a person, kiss them and kill them at the same time. That is the devil, I am telling you. But I am using my life to show you what I have learned about me from feeding on the word of God.

You might accurately think that I was a terrible person but I am only now willing to shock some and refresh others for the sake of those that are still trapped in places where I have been. There are people out there who think that to decapitate and dismember a body is not a horrifying thing. There are people in our midst that live totally devoid of any love of God being manifested in their life in any way that they can recognize. As impressionable youth, they are ignorantly adapting to the same kind of life that I did. As Christians, we are commissioned by God to do something about it. It can and does get very ugly.

There are many teachers among us like my teacher Joe K. These instructors/role models represent the same satanic powers and principalities that helped shape my life. These unknowing students need to see Jesus in us the survivors: the redeemed. This is another reason I believe this book is necessary.

Most of those who have been where the path of my life has taken me do not and/or cannot write books or talk about these things; the world usually only gets to see the fruit of their poisonous teachings. Joe came into my life at a time when I was a captive, receptive audience (i.e., a sponge). His cell was three doors from me (i.e., easy access). I esteemed his company and hungered for his ministry of death. On a daily basis, I fed on his words and instructions. In nearly twenty years of incarceration, he had read a lot. He familiarized me with semantics.

You see, there is a language of death. There is a demeanor of death. There is a spiritual familiarity that exists whereby like-spirited people can sense and sometimes even identify and recognize each other. For His own purpose, God saw fit to spare me. I told the Lord that I would never forget what He has done for me and I will never forget it. I praise Him today. For me, He is indeed the way, the truth and the life.

Chapter 11: *Peek-a-boo With Death*

This is one of the times I am convinced that I came close to being killed in the streets. I only became aware of this episode years after it happened. The incident involved some people whose names I can't mention. I will describe it as best I can, but in deliberately vague terms. I don't like to really tell this, but it may yet serve to glorify God by illustrating just where He brought me from.

In 1980, I was married to the mother of my two sons. We lived in Highland Park, Michigan. I had reacquainted myself with some people that I knew from prison. The people I knew were closely connected with a big drug dealer around Detroit known for his cold blooded brutality. His name I cannot mention. Because of the way my prison experience was regarded, I gained the respect of one of his top lieutenants. After meeting and talking with me, he decided to give me $200 worth of dope - about twenty packs.

I had the dope for about an hour before being approached by narcotics officers. I managed to throw the packs out of my personal possession, but the cops found them anyway. It seemed quite strange that I wasn't arrested on the spot. A few days later, they came back and asked me about the dope. They told me that the quality of my dope was much stronger than everything else being sold in the area. I had nothing to say. I knew that to tell on this dope man would mean certain death for me.

I didn't talk and the people that I was dealing for heard about it. At that point, they gave me $500 worth of dope; they gave me enough to support my own dope habit and make a few dollars. They gave me the five bundles (fifty packs) and I got high. I ultimately shot up all of the dope and had made no money; that was not good. When they asked for their money, I gave them a story to stall for time. I had some cousins that the big dope man knew very well. Because the boss knew and respected my cousins, they gave me more time to pay my debt, but after awhile, that got old too. They wanted their money and I couldn't produce it.

We had a meeting at my cousin's house and another meeting about their money by phone. I never told them, but one night I got high with the woman of a guy that I used to hang out with. He was in prison. She and I shot up all of the dope. I told the dope men that I knew a woman who owned some valuable jewelry. This was the same woman with whom I had shot up all the dope, mind you. My plan was for us to rob her so that I could pay what I owed. At this time, I was married and my first son was an infant. One night, the two lieutenants came by to pick me up for the robbery. I had called the woman's house to make sure she was there; I told her that I wanted to visit. We would rob her. I would pay them what I owed and be off the hook, so I thought.

The two men that came to pick me up raised pit bull dogs they fought for money. I called this woman's house, but no one answered the phone. Strangely, no one answered the phone. While I continued attempting to make contact, my wife came into the living room area. She met them and then went back into the bedroom with our child. What eventually occurred was that we didn't go since no one ever answered the phone. The dope men decided instead to go to the pit bull fight they had previously planned on attending. I was invited to go, but declined.

Less than ninety days later, these two men were charged with multiple homicides in connection with decapitations and body dismemberment. One of them, along with other co-conspirators, was convicted of the murder of three people. I knew the people that were killed and I knew that their monetary debts were no greater than mine. Their debts may not have even involved as much money, but they were killed, dismembered and decapitated. The case was big news around Detroit for a number of years.

Three people were dismembered and decapitated by these two men that I thought were coming with me to help me repay my debt to them. About two years later, after all of these guys were locked up, I saw another acquaintance. She was the woman of one of the men that came to my house that night. I knew her pretty well, so we talked as we occasionally saw each other in different places around town while chasing dope.

One day, she stopped me and our conversation got around to the point where she recognized that I really didn't know what was going on that night. She told me that the night that the two men came to my house - the night I thought we were going to stick up someone else - I was never going to make it to the stick up. They hadn't come for the robbery, but to kill me. I was shocked.

I deliberately remember that episode periodically. Every time I get the feeling that I was so tough and that I was such a gangster out there; every time I start thinking that I was somebody, I take myself back to the remembrance of that night. I think about what was really going to happen to me that night. I remember how vulnerable I was. I was perfect prey to be smashed like a bug at anytime in the midst of my foolishness. My poor wife and son would be victims by association.

But, I cannot close out this segment without acknowledging the grace and the mercy of God again . Only by His mercy and grace am I here to say I know He has a special place in His heart for fools like me. I have been chief of fools. I was in the sites of two cold-blooded killers that I knew personally. They could and would have scratched my name off the list of the living without a second thought. God only knows why He saw fit to let me live to write this book. He alone knows why He chose to spare my stupid life.

Chapter 12: *Chief of Fools*

This incident occurred in the 80's in Detroit while I was still chasing drugs. I was driving accompanied by one other person. We went to a drug house. Our money was short that day, but we spent everything we had buying heroin. After shooting our dope, we were just sitting there talking jive. The doorman had a single barreled shotgun broke down and he was putting a shell in the chamber before closing it. He was standing facing me as I sat on the couch. I had a policy of telling everybody to not aim a gun at me neither empty nor loaded.

To do so, I threatened, meant consequences from me. If he closed the shotgun, it would be aimed directly at me head.

Before he closed it, I told him again that nobody aims a gun at me, empty or loaded. I told him that I was prepared to act like he was deliberately trying to shoot me and I, too, had a gun. He turned from me in the living room and faced the direction of the dining room. As he closed the gun, it went off. The buckshot went through the first wall and penetrated the wall on the other side of the dining room about fifteen feet away. In the panic, we all ran from the dope house thinking somebody would call the cops because of the gunshot. We left the apartment for at least a half hour to see if the cops would come. We sat in our cars to see what was going on until we were convinced the cops weren't coming.

We went back into the apartment. Examining the scene, everybody could see that the height at which the shotgun shell expended itself was exactly at the level of my head. Needless to say, had he closed that gun standing in front of me, he would have blown my head off. I will never forget that. Ironically enough, in the mist of all that, I only considered his carelessness as it related to my getting some free dope from him. I tried, but it didn't work. Only God knows the possible value of telling about this shameful and deplorable period of my life.

Chapter 13: *A Different Side of Allen*

I have learned that the Lord has put certain attributes in me that I am only now beginning to understand. I believe that the gifts and talents that He gives a person are meant to be developed by Him. The people and situations I am going to talk about are memorable to me because they represent milestones in learning who I am.

I met Dominic on the east side of Detroit as a teenager. He was seeking the affections of a teenage girl in the neighborhood. The girl's brother was my best friend.

Dominic was born in Sicily and his father was a very prominent figure in the Detroit underworld. They also had a lot of money. On two occasions that I know about personally, he wrecked cars that his parents bought for him. After the wreck, he simply made a phone call and someone delivered a new car right to the scene of the accident.

Dominic's attempt at getting this girl's attention was unsuccessful because the girl liked me. It never caused a problem between us, however, and I always considered Dominic to be a friend. He was like a part of the family since his pursuit of this girl caused him to be around a lot.

Dominic grew up on the east side in a predominantly black environment and he identified with black people. He even got his hair processed, though his hair was naturally straight. His identification with blacks in the hood never wavered. But he and I didn't develop a close relationship until we were incarcerated together in Jackson.

He was sentenced to seven to fifteen years for armed robbery. He robbed a big dope man of a large quantity of dope. Because of his felony conviction, he was classified as an illegal immigrant; he had never become an American citizen.

Dominic had a hard time adjusting to prison life. He appeared vulnerable to other prisoners. He was approached by some of the predators and attempts were made to bully him. Dominic and I developed a close relationship resulting from the security provided by the people that I knew. Being protected by his association with our group caused others to stop bothering him. He eventually became a marathon runner while doing his time once he was relieved of the threat of being attacked. But while in Jackson, we talked a lot and we became friends.

As he approached the end of his minimum sentence, the federal government brought a deportation charge against him. The final judgment of his case was that he was to be deported to Sicily. After serving four years of his minimum sentence, he was taken to the airport from Jackson Prison and sent back to Sicily. The authorities were well aware who his father was, so when I received a correspondence from him from Barcelona, Spain, I became the focus of some severe scrutiny by the department of corrections. I was nothing but a little obscure mediocre pimple; a common dope fiend, street thug wannabe. I was a legend only in my own mind. I was doing life already and as far as I was concerned, they couldn't hurt me anymore.

I mention Dominic because I considered him a friend. He was the kind of person that would voluntarily do what he could to help you if he recognized your need. You didn't have to ask for help from Dominic if he knew you needed it. That is a rare quality. I don't and have never regarded a lot of people as my friends because most people do not qualify. Most people don't have what it takes to be a friend, but Dominic proved himself to be that kind of a person and I will never forget him. I just hope that he will find his way to the arms of grace and receive God's mercy just as I have.

There is a recurring theme here that will illustrate a pattern that keeps coming up in my life. I went to jail for homicide because I was standing up for somebody who wouldn't stand up for himself. I came to characterize myself as being an "other folk's fighter." I have been fighting for other folks all my life. I am just really learning to understand myself as I am coming to understand the love of God. A desire to learn of Him is the kind of relationship that He desires to have with every one of us.

This next incident occurred in 1969. I was still working at the automotive plant. I had experienced the heroin, but it had not completely taken over my life yet. I had my hair fixed; I had my Cadillac and a pocket full of money. I thought I was all that and a bag of chips, as the young folks say.

It was a summer night. I was walking down the street just after dark near my mother's house on the east side. In our neighborhood at that time, you could leisurely socialize outdoors on warm summer nights, and besides, my family had been living on this street for fifteen years. It was a close knit neighborhood and I knew almost everybody.

As I walked down the block, I saw this little boy sitting on the steps crying. It was around 10 p.m. I asked the little boy what was wrong and he told me that his mother had made him sit outside on the porch. I asked him why and he told me that he didn't know why. I asked him if it was a punishment and the little boy said no. I asked where was his mother and he said she was in the house.

I knocked on the door. The lady answered and let me step inside. Standing in the living room I could see a man lying on the couch. The mother was sitting on the side of the couch kidding around with the man. I asked her if she knew that the little boy was on the porch and she said yes. I asked her why and she said that she didn't want to be bothered with him right then. I told her that her little boy was outside scared and crying. She yelled out to him to shut up. I lost it.

The man on the couch jumped up and started to tell me to be quiet. So, I pulled my gun and told him to sit down and shut up. He did. Then, I told the lady to bring the little boy in the house. She asked who I was and threatened to call the police on me. At that point, I started crying and told her that she couldn't treat the boy that way or call the police on me. I took over her house, but by that time, someone had called my mother.

My mother asked me to leave; I was crying. I was furious and I didn't know who to take it out on. I wonder about episodes like that because they have happened more than a few times in my life. I believe that these volatile and violent expressions were perversions of what was meant to be used by God to show compassion. My expressions were very inappropriate. I believe the origin of some of my behavior was from not being properly trained in the things of God. Had I known how to observe a measure of restraint and wisdom, I may have possibly accomplished what my heart wanted to accomplish. I obviously didn't know how. I am only now learning that God is able to provide me with the much needed anointing to do what I failed to do that summer night in 1969.

The next person is a Muslim woman named Zana. I met her under unusual circumstances. I was riding down the expressway during a snowstorm. She was in a small 4 wheel drive SUV. Her car had hit ice and went into a skid. She had hit the center divider between the northbound and southbound traffic. Her car was completely stopped. She was far enough ahead of me in traffic that I was able to stop before hitting her.

She was seated behind the wheel, but not moving. Her head had apparently hit the steering wheel in the crash. She was now slumped over the steering wheel unconscious. Fortunately, traffic was not very heavy. I removed Zana from her car, took off my long leather coat and laid her on the ground on my coat. The approaching traffic was blocked by my car. Another driver somehow was able to get out of his car to assist me.

With his cell phone he made the call to EMS. For a short while, the southbound I-75 traffic was totally blocked off and backed up. I could have quite easily been killed, but I was not hurt. However, Zana was badly hurt and was rushed to the hospital. A few weeks later, I was contacted by her family. They told me that she was partially paralyzed and that both legs were broken. Someone during the subsequent investigation questioned why I moved her. That made me angry because I know I was only trying to help her.

Still, I went to see her in the hospital. (She was unable to walk

107

for almost a year.) I also went to see her in rehab and found out that she had two small children, she was engaged to be married and she was an airline stewardess. A practicing Islamic who lived in Dearborn, Zana had been returning home from one of the family businesses in Hamtramck when the accident had occurred.

I later accepted an invitation to meet her family in Dearborn. My brother went along with me. The reception by her family proved to be pretty much what I had expected; veiled hostility particularly from the males. I never met her fiancé, but in our talks over the phone, she surprised me with her observation that I had visited her more than her fiancée. His business involvements had somehow kept him from coming to see her. She eventually cancelled the wedding.

I was also really heavily using drugs at this time. I knew that she was grateful, but there was something else about the way she explained herself and her feelings about canceling the wedding that intrigued me. It crossed my mind that maybe I was possibly becoming an object of her affections. I made sure that I let her know that I was a Christian. She was very kind towards me. I know that she was consciously aware of the cultural taboo that she could be threatening, but she seemed almost willing to say "forget the taboos." I think that she may have confused gratitude with something else.

I kept my distance from her because I was well aware of my lifestyle as a dope fiend. I really didn't have any room in my life for anybody else. I knew she wouldn't be an enabler, so I stayed away. Still, I thought about her a lot (and maybe someday I'll get the chance to tell her thank you for helping to save my life).

In 1996, she was pursuing litigation against her insurance company following the accident. I was never able to connect with her to make a deposition on her behalf with her attorneys. She eventually dropped the lawsuit. That was the end of our contact for awhile until one day I did call her. By this time, I had been kicked out of every drug treatment center in Detroit that I knew of. One week before the call to Zana my mother had given me a dollar and a quarter to catch the bus to Harbor Light Treatment Center. From there I rode a bus to Harbor Light Treatment Center(My mother couldn't trust me in her house, so she gave me bus fare through the door.)

I had stayed in Harbor Light for five days to detox. While there, supposedly to detox, I had made $8 selling the pills they gave us to help make withdrawal less painful. It was enough to buy a pack of dope. I left Harbor Light after five days and immediately bought some dope.

Somewhere in the process, I glimpsed my despicable circumstances again. I called an administrator that I knew at the Detroit Rescue Mission Ministries. I asked him if he could help me get back into the program there. For some reason, I thought about Zana and I called her. In our conversation, I expressed to her how on our initial acquaintance, I had saved her life. I told her that I knew she was very grateful but today I needed her to help me save my life. She asked what it was that I needed and I told her that I needed $50. She asked me where I was and I told her where to meet me. She said she didn't have the money, but assured me she would get it. Sure enough, she did meet me with the money as planned.

I took the money, went to the dope house and got high. As I

was getting high, I could feel that something strange was going on. I didn't understand what was happening to me, but I knew something was happening. I thought that I was dying. I had asked and had been accepted into the treatment program before I got Zana's money, but I had bought dope with the money instead.

Chapter 14: *Homeless*

The homeless period of my life began when I burned my last bridge. After having violated everybody else that I knew, I stole from my mother's home a combination TV/radio and was too ashamed to go back. From 1995 to 1997, I lived in abandoned houses, junk cars and homeless shelters. I now had a drug addiction that had progressed over a period of more than twenty years.

By the end of 1995, I had lost a final job assignment. I couldn't support my methadone, heroin, alcohol and crack habit anymore. Now, through my jaded perception of desperation, I had stooped to stealing from my mother (i.e., the only person in the world who had never turned me away). The only place I knew to go was the Cass Corridor.

When I left my mother's home that night, I never dreamed that I would ever live in vacant buildings. My mind told me that everything was going to be all right and that I would be back on top of things again like so many other times. I would get some more money, get another job and/or find another woman to enable me. But God had another plan. Life during that period was really bad, to put it mildly.

Finally, I could not fall back on my parents support. I won't call what they did enabling because they were not trying to protect me from myself. When I would come by and ask them for money, usually in small amounts, they usually didn't deny me. Of course, they knew where all of my resources were going. Everybody could see what my money was being spent on. But I can't blame my parents for loving me. They were in a precarious, very ugly situation. Because of their love for me, they unwillingly tolerated a son that was trapped in the jaws of a demon. The devil had control over me! It was something that they couldn't begin to understand.

I will never know how bad it must have been for them. I can only imagine how their heart must have been repeatedly broken. The son they loved and who had brought them so much delight and pride in the past was now a derelict/bum on skid row. In the only world they knew about, I was as low as a man can go without being dead. They had a very ugly hand dealt to them by me. But looked at another way, my life was yielding predictable consequences. I was reaping what I had sown.

My new 'home' became the Cass Corridor and the nearby old Brewster Projects. I lived in a room in a vacant apartment with homeless guys on the 14th floor of one of the buildings. Many nights a dog would also come up to the room to sleep just as we did. The dog used one of the two bedrooms for a toilet just as we had. In these vacant apartments, when the water was turned off, squatters would use the toilets until they were full. And like us, the dog would not sleep in the toilet room. I was literally living like a dog with a dog.

We took an elevator to get to the room. Sometimes I wonder if the dog took the steps every night to the 14th floor or did he too take the elevator. Who knows? We would hustle for food during the day to have something to eat in our room at night. This was our temporary home. A couple of the guys were on fixed incomes receiving checks once a month. Others had incomes coming in from different places. Everyone received food stamps and everyone hustled to support their habit. We used to talk about our plans for the next day. We spoke of the check we were expecting or the kind of crime that we were going to commit. I remember one guy in particular who was on SSI (supplementary security income). A lot of homeless people on SSI were on it because they were drug addicts or mentally impaired, but nobody ever admitted to being crazy. Every SSI recipient had supposedly "fooled" the psychiatrists into thinking what they wanted them to think. Got it!

But looking back on it, all of us were crazy - even certifiably crazy - but we didn't know it. We lived there for months. It was strange how we became used to certain people coming into those vacant apartments and we expected them to be there. Everyone had different times that they would show up. If a guy didn't show up in a few days, we would start asking about him. Is he dead? Is he in jail? Is someone looking for him? We expressed an interest in almost a caring way because we expected each other to be there. There was no "expectation" that anyone had found a job or that anyone had moved to his own apartment or anything like that. We had adapted to this lifestyle and we all knew it.

I would have never said it, but I did recognize that I could get stuck there and die there. I knew that I didn't want to die like this. I knew that I shouldn't be there; nobody should live like that. I needed to get out of there but I didn't know how. Part of my dilemma was that not once, not even for a minute, did I ever consider not using dope anymore. (I know there is a devil, and that is one of the ways that I know.) The most obvious thing that contributed to my life being brought to this point - the most common factor - was substance abuse and yet I couldn't see it. There was never any remote reference to drugs being the root of our problem by anyone. Everybody would talk about quitting our drug use as if it was a simple choice. "I can stop anytime I am ready." Or, "Let me get my life together and then I will stop using drugs."

It sounds insane, but this was a common response among the people that I was around. I know that this uniform denial syndrome exists. I have been around dope fiends for over forty years. Therefore, these threads of information may hold potential benefits for those still in bondage.

It would be worthwhile for some readers to consider what I am talking about here. My experience could possibly help you find a way out. I pray that these dark and shameful disclosures will shed some light on the matter for someone. If exposing my miserable life does not reveal hope to someone that there is a way out , then I am wasting everybody's time. But I know without a doubt that the way out is through a man named Jesus.

Talking about my life in abandoned houses is not easy. These are very painful memories. I can remember not caring about observing personal hygiene habits. What was the need? I would wake up with sleep in my eyes, no toothpaste, no comb, no soap and water. So what? What difference did it make? I remember just not caring. I would go outside and look at people knowing that they looked at me like I was a piece of filth. I looked bad, smelled badly, and when I talked, I sounded bad, but it didn't make any difference.

Something else significant also occurred during this time in my life that is hard to talk about. My life was so desolate of almost everything civilized. In the rebuilding process going on right now, I am learning to appreciate things that really matter. When different social, public and even private things come up, my first reaction is usually to ask the question, why? I usually question things that most people take for granted. Most of the time, I will agree with the answer. I don't just accept things just because people are doing it or just because that is the way that it has always been. My experiences have enabled me to have a greater appreciation for some of the things that do matter as well as a more discriminating eye for the things that don't. There are too many social protocols that people observe, just because. I know that, in fact, many of them just don't matter. It impedes getting God's work done.

I am really cautious about saying this, but I thank God that I know that there are a lot of extravagances socially that could be distractions to me, but because of my past life, they are not. I believe that aspects of my miserable life have benefited my walk with God and with my Beverly. We are less distracted and can more effectively do what I call "cut through the fat meat." We get right to the business of being about our father's business. I deliberately choose not to look around at what other believers and Christians are doing because of how it compels me to ask questions.

I was a dope fiend that progressively grew to a point of worshiping drugs as my god for over twenty years. I have only been serving Him and growing in Him since 1997. So, when I see what others are doing now, I question what were they doing all those years when I was a dope fiend. I deliberately try not to look at this because I know that my only hope is that God will fulfill His word in me.

I must learn to be obedient to Him. He has given me much and much is required of me. He has taken Beverly and I to a place where we must deal with His business for us. That is my heart. I am not saying that I am the only one, but I can talk about me. The story of my life is what I can offer in part to the benefit of somebody. I am really talking about how I am being benefited by God. I do not have to totally be accurate with this. I have subjected myself to a lot of unnecessary and compelling misery. This is what it took for me. If this book is ever brought to the point of being published, there will be those who are yet to encounter many of the things that I speak about. There will be others who hopefully may never have to go as far as I did, but there will also be many who have already gone beyond the kinds of things that I am talking about without realizing it.

Maybe the tragedy of my past will help to stabilize baby Christians in their new found liberty. We need help as infant Christians in learning to follow Him as we become more fervent in serving Him. There is a sin sick world out there that needs us. The battle is raging and we need to be equipped as soldiers to prevail against the enemy. Being in an abandoned house is not the same as being in jail. It is not like being in a circumstance where you cannot defend yourself in anyway. I have seen people that were crippled and diseased.

I remember seeing Freddie let maggots consume the poison from his abscesses right outdoors in downtown Detroit (on John R. and Adelaide in the park). He was told that the maggots would only eat the poison from his sores. I have seen some ugly things out there.

Casey had a sore on his foot. He was a homeless man, so he kept his boots on all winter. When he removed his boot, his foot remained in the boot: gangrene had set in. He was taken to the hospital and both of his feet were removed at the ankle. I went to see him in the hospital. He was still smiling and anxious because he couldn't wait to get out of the hospital to get his next drink. I don't know what became of him after that.

I know people like Alfonso who was a crack addict. He had what I call a confused sexual orientation. He was treated badly by men. He exposed himself voluntarily to sexually transmitted diseases by submitting to the urges of other homeless men. This was his way of being accepted.

Men in these circumstances oftentimes resort to whatever means convenient to express themselves sexually with anybody and anything. After one of these encounters, Alfonso was beaten badly and left in one of the abandoned buildings. He received frost bite resulting in double amputation of his legs at the knee. He is wheel chairing around downtown Detroit today panhandling (begging). He is also dying of AIDS. It is a sad thing.

These are small glimpses of the ravages that sin can manifest. When the devil gets a foot hold he will ultimately take your life. These kinds of horrors were common in those places. Somehow, it seems strange to me now to hear of people doing what we used to do in crack houses. I thought I should have been the last lost slave/fool. We were looking for love in all the wrong places. I didn't know that back then even though I used to say it all the time.

There were even couples in some vacant buildings. They considered themselves to be in committed relationships. I also know of places where squatters have climbed the utility pole

117

and activated the electricity. They thought nothing of risking getting burned to death. They were actually trying to make homes in these vacant buildings with no running water. This occurred, by the way, right in downtown Detroit.

I thank God for Jesus. I thank Him for His sacrifice and for the forgiveness of my sins. I thank Him for just being patient with me and seeing me through my walk through my dark valley. He is the only reason I was able to come through this place. He is the reason I can represent hope to a hopeless somebody in need; somebody with the willingness to hear and a heart to receive; somebody ready to recognize that until the Lord speaks into your life, it ain't over yet.

I lived in an abandoned building in Highland Park across the alley from my mothers' home. At all costs, I didn't want her to know. I remember one evening I asked her for a blanket. At that point, I was able to keep my clothes clean and look presentable enough so that it didn't look like I was homeless. She gave me this handmade quilt that was worth about $400. This was a one-of- a - kind quilt that she gave me. I remember going to that vacant building that night. I could only stay there for a couple of days because the young dope boys were selling dope during the day from the building.

They were using the building for a stash and true to form, even though I told them why I was there and what I was doing, in their own shenanigans, one of them saw the opportunity to steal something and blame it on the crack head upstairs. That is exactly what they did. I had to leave there in haste to keep from getting shot, beat down or killed. I had to leave that very beautiful blanket in there. If it was not found by someone beforehand, it was lost when the building was eventually torn down.

I remember once walking over two miles because a dope man said he would give me a free sample of heroin. I went to the location and waited half the day. He did give samples, but the dope was not strong enough to keep me from going through withdrawals. I couldn't think of anything else to do, so I had someone call EMS. I was thinking that I could go to the hospital and get some free dope of some kind to help take the edge off. The EMS took me to Grace Hospital on Detroit's west side. They gave me a prescription that I had no money to fill. They put me out of the hospital around 1 a.m. I was stranded at least five miles from Highland Park. Having no money I started walking. After walking for an hour, I was tired and weak along with experiencing withdrawal pains.

I had learned how to sleep in a cardboard box. The night that I learned that trick, I slept right in the middle of downtown Detroit in Kennedy Square. A guy taught me how to do this by taking two large cardboard boxes and pulling them together so that no air gets inside. (The body will generate enough heat to keep you warm.) This night it was not very cold and I had on a light jacket. I awoke the next day having spent my first night in a cardboard box.

I went to work the following morning at a job in a small welding shop near Detroit. But on this particular night I found a box and I climbed behind the bushes on the side of someone's house. I cut a hole in the box so that I could see when the sun was coming up. This way, I could get out before people came out and had me arrested.
I was in a nice neighborhood. I woke up and walked back to the familiar neighborhood. My "home" was an abandoned

building in Highland Park with a homeless acquaintance named Geno. He had used a penny to bypass the fuse box so we could have electricity. We slept on old mattresses we found in the alley. Before long, we noticed a burning smell. It was the object being used to bypass the fuses. The building eventually burned down and we had to find another place. We just went around the corner to another building.

In the morning, I used to sit behind the garbage dumpster at the Coney Island on Hamilton Street. I would look for potential victims; anyone that I could lie to or rob to get my dope. After I got it, I would go to this old abandoned apartment building and shoot my dope. There was an old mattress on the floor that I would sit on to shoot it. I remember getting up from the mattress one night after shooting my dope and preparing to leave. I had no idea where I was going. I thought to myself, since I don't have a home, why not just lie back down and sleep here? So I did.

A primary consideration about the choice of a particular abandoned house for the night was whether there was any open food close by. If food was around, you had to worry about being bit by a rat. A lot of people live like that now and most of those people, unfortunately, won't ever read this story. You see, this is not merely my story. The message is simple, but very few of those who experienced this life will live to tell their story. The message is that you don't have to die like you are living. The solution is much simpler than that. The good news is that you are not alone. Believe in, trust in and surrender to the name of Jesus.

Chapter 15: *1996 - The Darkest Hour*

Just before I acknowledged my deliverance from a twenty-seven year addiction to drugs, I experienced the lowest point in my life. The only reason that I wasn't fired from my job is because a journeyman can't be fired. As a journeyman millwright being assigned jobs through the union hall, an employer could only lay me off. I would then call the hall, await or find another assignment and go to work.

My drug habit had reached a level where I was taking 80 mg of methadone a day at a cost of $80 per week. At the same time, I was still shooting $100 a week in heroin. Between smoking crack, shooting heroin and drinking alcohol, I also spent another $100 a day. The methadone doses only cancelled my physical need for heroin.

When I got laid off from my job, I could no longer support my drug habit. I was then evicted from my rented house. Because I didn't know the exact day scheduled for the eviction, I happened to show up just after my belongings were set on the streets. Unfortunately, I lived on a street where my sons frequented. They spent a lot of time in that neighborhood and were well known. I actually became aware of this house through my sons. The public spectacle of my eviction caused them to suffer great embarrassment.

I arrived at the house before the neighbors could go through my belongings. I was able to get my coat, some of my personal clothes and a few other items. I went back to my mother's house where, as I mentioned earlier, I stole her combination radio/TV. Therefore, I couldn't go back there anymore.

I went to the Cass Corridor and took my seat at NSO. I was a common junkie on skid row. I contacted Bobby, a distant relative who was living in an apartment above a crack house on the east side. He was able to maneuver me a place to sleep. A bunch of addicts lived upstairs there, in fact. One crack head was officially the renter. The rest of us just squatted. I was paying him $25 a week when I had it, but he accepted anything we gave him, especially crack.

It was a cold winter in 1995. This house was across the street from where I grew up on the east side of Detroit. I could look out the second story window of the crack house and see the empty lot where my childhood home used to be. I have some very painful memories of this horrible time in my life. I was strung out, broke and hopeless. I had nothing but a dope habit. I had shamefully despised my parent's home. I had no friends. I couldn't go in front of my family. I was just out there. Of course, I didn't know that I was right at the end of my living hell. I had no clue that I was at the door of my new life.

I can recall the mornings when the hunger was so intense that none of the dope heads in the house could take it anymore. On those days, we would walk from the dope house we lived in to the soup kitchen; it was about a thirty minute walk. I recall how a bunch of us would go there for a meal. Some of the guys would carry bags to bring food home. We would try to scrounge up on enough food to get us through the rest of the day. We knew that the money we had would be spent on drugs, but we also knew we would be hungry later. We knew that we would only have a once a day chance to get free food. I didn't want to be seen carrying food around like the bum that I was. Sometimes as we walked, I would fall behind the group. Even in my downtrodden state, I remember very clearly that I still vainly called on the Lord. I didn't know what or if it was going to do any good, but sometimes out of sheer desperation, I would do it. I remember one song that I used to sing: It was, "Cast me not from your presence, Oh Lord! Take not your spirit from me. Return to me the joy of my salvation, and renew a right spirit within me." As I sang that song, I would cry silently. I had to make sure that I dried my tears before I caught up with the macho group.

Sixteen years had gone by since my experience with God in that upper room. I had walked away before I became rooted. I had gone back like so many weak babies. I had gone back to feed some more on my life of vomit. I state it this way because consistent with scripture, that's exactly what I did. Between the world, the devil and my contribution, my plate was again full of my own vomit. I had dined from that plate for the past sixteen years. I would sorrowfully think of that cleanness sixteen years later as I walked to that soup kitchen to get something to eat in the morning. This meal would very likely be the only meal I would eat that day.

I'd be walking singing that song – Psalm 51. This is the psalm that David wrote after he repented before God for arranging the murder of one of his personal friends. David wanted to hide the fact that he had sex with his friend's wife and that she was pregnant by him. He did a lowdown terrible thing. Uriah was his main man. Uriah wasn't just a common soldier in David's army. He was a personal friend of David's, so much so that to sleep in King David's castle was no big thing.

While Uriah was out fighting for David in the war, David was having sex with Uriah's wife. David tried to cover this up by having Uriah come home to have sex with his wife in hopes that Uriah would think the baby was his. But Uriah was so devoted to David that he would not even go home. His reason being that he would feel bad knowing that as a soldier he was enjoying himself while his comrades were out there risking their lives in battle.

When David could not cover his sin, he ordered Uriah to be killed. He hoped to compromise Uriah's integrity. He hoped Uriah would go against his own will so that David's sin would be covered up, but it didn't work. David finally used one of his army generals – a cousin – to set his friend Uriah at the most dangerous part of the battle where he was killed.

David concealed his scheme until he was exposed by a prophet. Alas, David acknowledged his sins before God and repented. This song was written as a song of repentance before God by King David. This man was out of God's will. He knew it and he asked for God's mercy. I was like that. I would be walking and singing that song on those weary days. I would be crying and my thoughts would be that, Lord, if you are out there somewhere, please do not let me die like I am living. Don't let me die like a dog. I am not afraid to die, but I do not want to die like this. Please! I couldn't know all that I had done wrong. I did know that I did not have a repentant heart. I was not acknowledging my sins. My crazy dope fiend way of thinking was that maybe I had got high wrong. I knew there were certain things that I had done that were undeniably wrong, criminal - even cruel. But a repentant heart – I did not have one yet.

I refuse to remotely imply in this book that I was some goodie two-shoes; that I saw a light or that I got right all at once. That would be a lie. The truth is that I did not acknowledge God's deliverance right away. In fact, I wasn't even thinking about God when the deliverance happened. All I did was cry out to him from that building in the Cass Corridor. After that prayer, I just continued my slow but sure death walk. I expected to die at any time. I just hoped that it wouldn't hurt much. I hoped it would be quick. I had shamefully despised everybody I knew and loved. I could expect no help from any human being. My appointment with a violent and disgraceful death was just a matter of time as far as I was concerned.

It was after my deliverance from dope that I began to question the possible association between my deliverance and God. This may not sound so religiously correct, but what matters is that this is how I can best describe what happened to me. Whatever way the Lord sees fit to use this story to His glory is alright with me. I don't care how he does it as long as He does it – that's fine. I am not looking for glory in this. I am blessed already. If nobody reads this book but David, Michael and my Beverly I don't even care. It's in God's hands now. He is the almighty sovereign God. He is the one who took the love and virtual worship of dope from my life and out of my heart. He replaced my former love for and worship of that demon with Himself. Any way that He wants to use the story of my wretched life is fine with me. I want to thank Him for giving me this opportunity to say thank you Lord.

Chapter 16: *COMAYA Ministries*

This is how COMAYA Ministries began on May 31, 1998. I acknowledge my physical deliverance from drugs on April 8, 1997. I had been homeless on the streets of Detroit for two years after I had stolen from my mother. I was too ashamed to go back to her home to look in her face. I was existing on the streets of Detroit in what is considered the skid row area known as the Cass Corridor.

The shelter that I most often frequented and have mentioned earlier was called the Neighborhood Service Organization - NSO. I recall something incredible that happened one night. There was an evangelist group that came to minister to us homeless people as we sat in our chairs. One member of the evangelist group was a very large Caucasian man. He testified that he was a former professional player with the Canadian football league. He also testified how he became entangled with drugs, was miraculously delivered and was now an evangelist. As he spoke, he had eye contact with me a couple of times. I was sitting in the NSO going through heroin withdrawals. I didn't feel well at all. I was just sitting there. He said, "Hey, you right there. God has something for you." He came down the aisle past other people and said to me, "God is going to use you."

I said, "Yeah, right!"

"You know it, don't you?

I said, "Yeah!" cause I knew in my heart that I did but I had abandoned that belief and had accepted that I was now beyond hope. I was more concerned with living through my immediate situation.

He said, "God is going to use you right in this place to bring people to Him. You have been knowing it awhile, haven't you?"

I said, "Yeah!"

"What are you doing about it?" he asked.

I said, "Nothing, man. I wish you'd get away from me and leave me alone."

"Okay! I am not going to bother you, but I just wanted to let you know what God told me."

"Yeah, right!" I said and I just went on being a dope fiend.

But scripture says, "And we know that all things work together for good to them that love God, to them who are called according to His purpose." I didn't love God because I didn't know Him. I talked about Him. I read about Him. I had heard about Him. I had even been on TV ministering about Him. I didn't know Him in the sense that I had never really trusted Him.

When the going got tough, I resorted to the thing that was most familiar to me - dope. I trusted my dope. It was predictable what my dope would do. It would make me numb to pain: emotional and otherwise. With dope as my companion, I believed that I could handle anything that the world could dish out. I had that kind of hopelessly deceived

127

confidence. But even as I speak, I am reminded of Proverbs 3:5-6. It says, "Trust in the Lord with all your heart." I didn't trust Him with all of my heart; not yet.

The NSO walk-in center had only recently set up a new project in the back room of the homeless shelter. It was designed to be a detoxification unit for strung out dope fiends like me. My little group was one of the first attempts at implementing this program. Sadly, it was discontinued shortly after I finished. But I believe now that God set it up for me to have a way of escape according to 1 Corinthians 10:13. I went through detox in the back room of the NSO for five days. At the end of the detox period, we had to make a decision. We could either go to Herman Kiefer Hospital to be processed into an extended treatment program or be released back into that hopeless, helpless, homeless jungle again.

In the dope fiend part of my mind, I was just going through a revolving door process. I was an experienced professional dope addict and I just wanted a place to go to rest up a little and dry out so I could get high cheaper. I figured I would have time to organize my thoughts enough to setup a new plan whereby I could continue to get high the right way this time. I also was in the NSO because I had been kicked out of every place else. I had been kicked out of COTS only days before. The workers at COTS smelled alcohol on my breath - a violation of policy punishable by immediate eviction. I was kicked out of the Detroit Rescue Mission Shelter because I got high after graduating from their treatment program but before being transferred to another program. I was kicked out of everywhere else I knew to go. I had nowhere to go but the NSO.

I went to Herman Kiefer after the five day detox at the NSO. The staff was assigning people to places for further treatment. They finally came up with the option that I could either stay out on the streets for the next thirty days or I could go to a place called SHAR-Day Treatment. When I heard SHAR, I knew automatically that I didn't want to go there. Every dope fiend knew that if you didn't want to get clean, you didn't want to mess with the SHAR house organization - period.'

The treatment center being offered as a last resort for me was associated with the SHAR house organization. They had a reputation for being serious about people getting clean and staying clean. I wanted nothing to do with that, but I had nowhere else to go. Then, I heard that it was a full care facility. They would attend to everything. We called it "three hots and a cot." I could count on a clean place to sleep and three meals every day. I would have to do all the treatment stuff, even though I surely didn't want to hear it. But I was trapped.

For the next couple of days, I was at the SHAR-Day Treatment Center. I don't think I was there a week when one morning I started to get real thirsty. The more water I drank, the more frequent I had to urinate. It got worse throughout the day. All that day, I was drinking what I know now to be a high sugar content soft drink that they had made for us. It tasted good and I was drinking a lot of it because my thirst was going crazy. I must have drunk two gallons of water that day. My urination frequency during that day went from every two hours to every thirty minutes by late that night.

That evening, I began to vomit. I was asked if I wanted to go to the hospital. I said, "No, I'm all right."

The vomiting progressed to where I just sat on the bathroom floor over the toilet. I would periodically get up, go to the sink, drink some water, go back to the toilet and throw up some more. I was suffering terrible stomach cramps. Forcing myself to vomit temporarily relieved some of the stomach pains and cramps. It felt to me like withdrawal and pancreatitis, but then every pain to me felt like heroin withdrawal. At this point in my life, the only thought about relief from pain, any pain, was like dope fiends get – you need more dope. I didn't know what was happening.

The day shift worker told the night shift attendant what my condition was. He came up and told me to put on my clothes: that I was going to the hospital. Nobody liked this guy because he was a hard guy with no flexibility. As I look back on the entire episode now, I believe he was instrumental in saving my stupid life. I didn't want to go to the hospital, but he wasn't taking no for an answer. I had had pancreatitis attacks numerous times before.

I was transferred from one hospital to another hospital. I was finally transferred to Detroit Receiving hospital where I remained for three days. In the hospital, I was given Demerol to reduce the severe stomach pains that accompany pancreatitis. Demerol is an opiate look- alike that would mask any opiates in my system. A urine test would indicate the presence of Demerol, which they knew the hospital was giving me for pain. I knew they would be unable to prove that I was high on heroin.

The day of my scheduled release from the hospital was also the day that I was eligible to receive my monthly stipend of food stamps. My dope fiend mentality went into gear. The head nurse on my hospital ward was a homosexual. Knowing how to manipulate him, I had him assist me in getting to my dope. I left the hospital, picked up my stamps, traded them for cash, bought dope, got high, and returned to the hospital before the head nurse contacted the treatment center staff to pick me up.

I returned to the treatment center conspicuously high. At the group NA meeting that night, I must have created quite a spectacle because the staff was really on my case. They repeatedly asked me if I were high. Convinced by my behavior that I was high, the staff conducted a hearing a few days later. At the hearing, they had the test results from a urine analysis. They asked me again had I used any heroin and I, of course, denied it. They sent me out into the hallway while they made their decision. Would they put me out of the treatment center without any proof other than their suspicions?

As I awaited their decision sitting in the hallway, I said to myself, "Well, Al. You tricked them again." But the question in my mind suddenly became who had really been tricked ? The answer was that it was me. Another question followed. Who had been the fool all these years? The answer again was me. Something happened inside of me in that hallway that day. I can't explain it. The closest I can come to explaining it is to say that something happened that only God could do inside of me that day. I felt the need to tell on myself. I wanted to snitch on me.

They called me back into the office. I asked them to stop the proceedings and allow me to speak before they made their final decision. I completely came clean to them about everything I had done. I pleaded to them to not put me out on the street because I wanted to be clean. They sent me into the hallway again. This was the first time since I began getting high on heroin that night at my uncle's house in 1969 - the first time in over twenty-seven years since I started sniffing heroin in my nose just experimenting - that I had ever told on myself. I figuratively got high once in 1969 and didn't come down until 1997. I was tired of being a fool and I said in my heart that I didn't want to die like a fool.

When I went back inside, three of the four staff decided that I should be put out. One counselor believed that he saw something in me. He pleaded with them for me based solely on his personal instinct. He had been the hardest core former dope fiend of the entire staff; I will never forget him. I thank God for him even as I speak because based on his pleadings, they agreed to offer me a contract. It included extra chores as a reprimand for my violation. It was my reprieve to stay in the program as long as I didn't violate any of the provisions of this contract.

I fulfilled my long list of obligations to the letter.

While still in the treatment center, one morning I awakened before the wakeup call. Before we ate breakfast and cleaned up the whole building, we had to clean our rooms. This morning, I was awakened by the Holy Spirit. I realized in an instant that the lust and love that had grown into virtual worship of the demonic forces that had witnessed my use of those drugs all those years was gone. I could feel it; I knew it. It was really gone.

I just started crying. I didn't know how it had happened. I thought maybe because of fear induced by the diabetes diagnosis I had become scared straight. Then I remembered a certain day in the Cass Corridor. I remembered a particular abandoned house where dope heads would shoot up and smoke dope. I remembered buying some dope after a day of hard hustling for the money. My veins over the years had become so depleted from shooting dope that I had to stick myself a lot of times to get the blood to back up. This was necessary so that I would know that I had the needle directly in line with the vein. When the blood would back into the needle, I could then shoot the dope.

I really had a lot of old tired veins, but I finally got the hit. All of a sudden, after I got high I just started crying. I had been flirting with death most of my life, but now that I could feel death's hot breath so near to me, and I knew that I would soon be dead, I just didn't want it to hurt. Sitting there on that milk crate I cried out to God:

"If you are out there somewhere, if you can do what they say you can do; I don't know if you are the God of Abraham. You might be anybody. I know what I read, heard and think. All I know is if you are around here and you can hear me, keep me from dying like a dog. I don't want to die like this. What about David and Michael (my two sons)? If you are around here, let me walk uprightly like a man just one day for them so they don't have to live with the thought that their dad died like a dog."

Thinking to myself, I thought, I have all this education, I went to the University of Michigan, I am a journeyman millwright, skilled trade's professional, I was smart in school, but here I

133

am dying like a dog ; a dope fiend in Cass Corridor. I didn't want that legacy for them. I was crying out to a God that I did not know. "Please don't let me die like a dog. This death is worse than a dog," I cried.

Standing on the streets sometimes I realized that if I did not make a lot of noise by convulsing and blocking traffic, nobody would have even cared. I knew that if I stood still right there on the streets of the Cass Corridor until I died, it would not have made any difference to anybody. And as I lay in that bed at that treatment center that morning, I realized that it was that prayer that had been heard by God and answered.

One day while living in the COTS Homeless Shelter, I went to buy some dope in the Brewster housing projects. It was winter and the ground was icy. On the way back as I looked for a place to shoot my dope, I slipped coming down this icy incline on the sidewalk. Because of a bad car accident in 1989, I had suffered multiple injuries and operations to my left leg. If I laid down on my back, I could not completely extend my left leg following the accident. On this particular day, I slipped and landed on my left knee. Miraculously, from that day on, I was able to fully extend my left leg.

I mention this incident because the Lord has also been a surprisingly unexpected fixer for me. Before I was delivered, I lived in the COTS Homeless Shelter in a room with three other guys. There were two bunk beds in the room. In one bed, there was a young man that had just been released from a psychiatric ward. He had attempted suicide and had severely burned his frontal torso. Because of this, he slept on his back, and he was very unstable acting. I don't know how it led up to

134

this, but at some point I led him in the prayer of repentance. Here I am a dope fiend in a homeless shelter leading someone to the Lord. I don't understand these things, but this stranger and I prayed the prayer of repentance and he accepted the Lord as his personal savior. I don't even know if I had the authority to conduct that prayer as an out of fellowship Christian myself, but I pray to God that he benefited from it. If his heart was right, then I am sure that the Lord did receive him. Wherever he is, if he is on this earth, I wish him well and I hope that he can spend eternity in the presence of the same God that I still serve every day.

I completed the process at the treatment center. By the time I was released, I was regarded as an honorable prospect. I was delivered from drugs and I knew it. As I was laying on my back that morning, I asked the Lord to let me know that it was Him that delivered me. I wanted to know what else could He do if he could do that. I wanted more. More has become the operative word that I have learned when dealing with the Lord.

Upon my release from the treatment center, with the staff's assistance, I entered a subsidized apartment. I understand now that the Lord was just babying me His immature child. And as I look back, I am so grateful. I promised Him that I would thank Him until the day that I die. I remind myself of how He blessed me in spite of my disgusting self.

But the lord has blessed me so good. I reconnected with my job at the union hall. I was given an immediate assignment to begin the Monday after my release from the treatment center on Friday. I was working seven days a week in ten hour shifts. My first paycheck was over $1,000. By the time I went to my first meeting scheduled for the people coming out of treatment, it was recorded that I was making too much money for them to assist me, but because of the unmerited favor of God, they chose to assist me anyway.

I didn't accept the allotment from them. I became isolated in the midst of the group since I was making in one paycheck more than everyone in that room put together. But I saved my money as I worked through 1997. I was seeking the Lord as I understood Him. I did not have a church home and I had not gone back to find my Beverly yet. I was too ashamed to even try. I was telling the Lord that he had blessed me so good by delivering me from that dope demon that I just wanted to serve Him and say thank you. I asked Him to just tell me what to do.

Someone had ministered a message over the radio that I had received in my spirit. The story was about a Hebrew man named Sham-gar. He single-handedly killed six hundred Philistine soldiers with an ox goad. (An ox goad is a big stick with a hook on the end used to control the movements of oxen.) A former football coach ministered the revelation he received from Sham-gar's experience. He put it in these terms: (1) Sham- gar started where he was; (2) he used what he had; and (3) he did what he could.

I embraced and acted on Sham-gar's example; that was enough for me. I told the Lord that I had saved my money. I had about $11,000. I said, "Well, it's all yours. It is to be used to glorify you." I made preparation as best I could to feed people. I decided to feed people in the park in front of my mother's house where the devil had made such a spectacle of me during my years as a dope fiend; I was going to feed people in the park.

I made all of the arrangements. I spent about $2,000. During that day, some miraculous things occurred. There was one particular woman who came out that day. I still have the note she wrote and handed to me during the feeding. I also established that day a relationship with a pastor whose congregation is on the corner near my mother's house. His church volunteered tables and chairs that day to help accommodate the need of the people being fed.

On that same day, I met a woman who also conducts a food ministry. Through her contact, I was supplied with meat, bread, and other food items for the next three years. Also that same day, a certain woman approached me. She had gone to the Marathon gas station nearby to ask for a notepad to write out her story. She told me that she had been in the alley behind my mother's house. She had broken a piece of glass and was going to cut her wrists to commit suicide. She had been raped many times and she was a prostitute. She was a drug addict and was in a methadone clinic. The man that was with her was dying of AIDS.

It was a hopeless situation she determined and she was about to give it all up when someone walking through the alley announced that someone was feeding people in the park. She stopped what she was doing and came to the park to eat. She shyly handed me this note. I read the note as she continued to apologize for giving me the note. At the same time, she was thanking me for helping to save her life. By now, being a reinstated cry baby, I just cried the rest of that day.

I also remember that after the feeding, my former counselor

showed up. He was the man who kept them from throwing me out of the treatment center. He came and ate barbeque with me at my mother's home. I was honored to serve him. He called himself a Sufist; something that I only knew was not a Christian. He had some kind of religious association, but it was not with Jesus. He gave me a name that he said came to him from his God. He called me a "righteous pillar." He told me that the name described how I would be used by God.

I didn't regard him as a spiritual man that could prophesy or do things like that, but he had seen something in me that caused me to not be put out of the center. As I sought the Lord as a baby Christian, He was pouring things into my spirit. I began to receive of Him as I progressively thirsted and hungered after Him. He deposited four words into my spirit: discretion, discrimination, moderation and respect. I received them with such enthusiasm. Initially, I assumed that God was giving me four ministry points to develop to go forth and use in my ministry, so I researched all of those words.

Since that time, they have repeatedly resurfaced in convenient as well as sometimes not so convenient ways in my walk with the Lord. Since the original imparting of these four words into my spirit, I have come to understand that they were not given to me primarily for ministry purposes. These four points have been useful to minister to me for my own personal growth and as I continue to grow, I keep referring back to these four words.

He gave me these points to help me grow in preparation for the future. I received them like a little kid. Even as you would tell a little kid, "You might not understand this now, but keep it on the inside of you and it will take root when it should," that is what is happening to me still. It has been a wonderful journey.

COMAYA Ministries was founded that day in the park. I was excited, I cried a lot and I still cry. Since that time, I have passed on the distribution of the food donation responsibilities to a pastor friend and other people. They pass out food to people in need on a daily basis throughout Detroit and Highland Park. It is not a large ministry, but we are just grateful that we are blessed to be a blessing. The name COMAYA Ministries came from the time when I was being assisted in my infancy by a former childhood acquaintance who is now a pastor.

After acknowledging my deliverance, I went back to the front line at the NSO. We began to minister there on a weekly basis. During one of our visits, as I was walking through the aisles talking to the people, I believe the spirit of the Lord impressed upon my spirit that I should call the ministry COMAYA; it is an acronym that stands for "Come As You Are." It is named COMAYA because I am convinced God came to the Cass Corridor personally and delivered me. He accepted me when I was filthy and despicable to myself, and everyone. I was not a positive contribution to anybody or anything. I contaminated everybody that I came into contact with, but He accepted me.

That is what He requires of me. He wants me to love the unlovable the same way that He loved me. That is where COMAYA Ministries began. That is the vision of COMAYA Ministries. We are not a real estate agency. My wife helped me to see that as well. We were blessed with some homes, but our objective and our mission is that we are blessed to be a

139

blessing and we are commissioned to love the unlovable. I would prefer not to have anything else to do with alcoholics, dope heads and drug addicts, but then who else can tell this story?

I am reminded of scripture references to why Jesus endured the pain of the cross. My bible teaches me how He identifies with the suffering of man by having endured suffering at the hands of men. He is alive and I know that he is alive because he lives in me. If it had not been for the Lord on my side, where would I be?

Chapter 17: *My Beverly*

"My Beverly." I could never love another after loving you. My life story could really be told under this heading. My Beverly has been the one immovable aspect of my life since she came into my life. I love her very much.

My first contact with Beverly was in the fall of 1969. She was a student at Eastern Michigan University (EMU) and we met casually through a mutual acquaintance. At that time, I was critically involved in Detroit street life. At twenty years old, after having been fired from my job, I was nothing more than a common street thug. The Cadillac car note that I was supposed to be paying, I would only pay when I had money. On most occasions my parents had to pay it. I became disgustingly irresponsible.

I lived in my parents' home amid the turmoil our family had become accustomed to. In 1970, my family moved from the east side of Detroit to a home in Highland Park. The family business was starting to wane. We still had a few after hour joints going and my father was still loaning money and both of my parents still had jobs. In my own foolish thinking, though, I thought I was living a gangster life. My denial was really just a not very good cover up for a boy disguised in a man's body.

My primary financial support was from my parents. I lived a lie. I stole, cheated and did whatever I could do to get money. I was a drug addict in denial. Periodically, I would visit Eastern Michigan's campus to visit my friend and go to parties, but I was not enthused with college life. I sold drugs to some of the students. I even involved a few of them in selling drugs for me. I had a sinister artfulness at entangling people in my unsavory affairs. A few students became strung out on drugs via their contact with me. Drug business eventually became my primary reason for being on campus.

I also remember going there to rob people. One particular night, we robbed this man whose family was returning from a vacation. We robbed him and took all of their luggage and money. We made him run from his own vehicle at gunpoint. We took all of the loot to Beverly's apartment. She had no idea at first as to what we had done. As we laid everything out on the floor of her apartment, I asked her if there was anything there that she wanted. She emphatically said no. She wanted nothing to do with any of that. She was appalled by what we had done. Today, I am so ashamed to even talk about it. That was the last contact I had with her at that point.

I came to know that Beverly grew up in a manner that I never thought existed. Her life, to me, was best depicted in the following old popular TV shows (i.e., Leave It To Beaver, Father Knows Best, My Three Sons, etc). Her family influence taught her to respect God and people, obtain an education, work hard, save money and enjoy life in a clean, honest way. Those virtues had no practical meaning to me. So I didn't really have any interest in her nor she in I.

Our next contact was three years later in 1973. I was doing life in Jackson Prison and according to her account, she was told by our mutual acquaintance about me. He told her that I was about to commit suicide. Many people on campus felt better after talking to Beverly. Even though our backgrounds were totally opposite, he thought maybe I too could benefit from communicating with her. I was, however, not about to commit suicide that way. I was just living the thug life in prison.

Another aspect was that from the point of our initial contact, my friend had always introduced me as being his older brother. Beverly believed that we were biological brothers. We started writing each other. When I look back on it, I believe that it was partially the desperation of my circumstance being met by her loving heart that made something happen during the course of our correspondence.
I didn't know that she was simultaneously making inquiries about me to these people she thought were my brother and mother.

She described me as intelligent and interesting. She was totally in the dark concerning my life as a criminal and substance abuser. The turning point for me came when I decided to take a chance and express my true feelings. Her words seemed so pure and filled with a love that I could not let get away. I had to tell her - whatever the cost. So, I took a step out and took the opportunity to talk to her about a man that was interested in a woman. I liked what I was reading and I was growing to love her.

What happened was at the exact time that I wrote that letter, she had just been told by my friend or someone in his family that I was supposed to be engaged to his sister. Our friend decided to tell her the truth about me not being his brother. She was told that upon my release, I would marry his sister. So, she had accepted that scenario. She told me that she was in the process of leaving my life by moving to another dorm when she received a phone call from me. Some may call it fate, but for the first time, I called her in the late evening instead of my usual time.

If I hadn't made the change, she would have moved without my knowing how to contact her. I, too, had grown close to her heart. That is how our love began. That was the first time that we ever expressed our interest in each other.

When I look back, my heart remembers some very unusual feelings. Beverly's love for me was the first time in my life that I fully believed that I was being accepted solely for who I was. In the world's terms, I had nothing to offer her.

I was twenty-three years old serving a life sentence in prison. The prospects statistically and legally for me to get out was slim to none. Judging by my record since being in Jackson, I was going to die there. Each year, lifers are reviewed. My record clearly indicated that the prison administration was surprised that I even made it to the review alive each year. They didn't expect me to leave Jackson alive because of my behavior alone - notwithstanding the life sentence.

I believe that God said no to me dying there or remaining there, but back to the matter of my Beverly. I don't feel like we fell in love; I feel that we grew in love. There was a part of each of our hearts that was open for this to happen. I know that her love filled a void for me. The part of me that was loved by Beverly had a sense of freedom. She took over my life with her love and I still feel that way. I enjoy her even more today.

We started corresponding more and expressing our real feelings for each other completely. She eventually came up and visited me and it grew to a point where she became my primary visitor. Prior to her visits, my mother had never missed a visiting day in all of those years. Beverly and my mother formed a very close bond that still exists today.

So many things happened. We made plans. My family was moving with their finances to get me out. Money was available to get me out when the right time came. About a year before we began our communication by mail, the so-called eye witness to the murder - the only other person in the hallway - submitted an affidavit recanting his earlier testimony. His new statement said that everything that he had said at the trial was a lie and that he had said it under coercion by police. He said that he felt that because of how the murder happened, I should not have to spend the rest of my life in jail. He would not accept any money from my family, even though it was offered. He just committed himself to filling out that recanting affidavit.

After that, I was encouraged and I was excited about the prospect of getting out. In my own mind, I felt like things were getting back in my control. Beverly embraced my belief in getting out in spite of everything. She was a young, beautiful woman – twenty-two years old. (She is still my Miss Fine.) She had obtained her Bachelor's degree from Eastern Michigan. She told me that I was instrumental in her decision to continue her education and pursue her Master's degree.

Between 1973 when we first started writing and my release in 1975, we went through many levels of growing deeper in love. She did all of the leg work to get me enrolled into University of Michigan on a full academic scholarship. We made plans while I was incarcerated to get married. She agreed to marry me while I still had life with no tangible prospect of my ever being released, but I chose to conspire with the Chaplin in Jackson to lie to her.

I told her that it was not permitted for me to get married because of my sentence. She accepted that. I felt that I loved her so much that I couldn't allow her life to be tied to mine in the unlikely event that I never got out.

During the time that I was making efforts to get out through the legal process, efforts were simultaneously being made for me to leave by other means if necessary. I knew that these other processes would put me in a status subject to killing people, being killed, and/or being a fugitive for the rest of my life. So, I believed that I was expressing a token of my love for Beverly by not binding her to me in marriage. I believed then and I believe now that if she would have married me and I had remained in prison, she would have been faithful. I believe that she would have been faithful, even though I doubt that I would have done likewise if the circumstances were reversed.

So, we made plans to be married upon my release. In January 1975, the Supreme Court gave me a reversal of my convictions. The conviction was set aside. This meant that my conviction was canceled. I was taken back to the trial court and given a new trial. In February 1975, I was transferred from Jackson to the Wayne County Jail. On July 8, 1975, my parents posted the money for my release on appeal bond.

But about six months prior to my release, before finding out that my appeal was successful, Beverly received the baptism of the Holy Ghost. She changed. Between the time that she received the Holy Ghost and my release on bond, we had come to the conclusion that we could not be married right away. I had not committed myself to her beliefs. Having accomplished her Master's degree from EMU, she was beginning her career as a teacher. She had an apartment in Ann Arbor.

I was released and was living at my parent's house. They had my Cadillac ready. They were involved at the time in selling hot cars, picking up numbers and the family business was doing well. Both of my sisters and my parents were driving new cars. They were doing business as usual. Everyone was dressed in diamonds and pearls. Beverly had arranged for me to start classes at the University of Michigan in the fall. Business was so good and as I became involved in the family affairs so quickly, I decided that I wasn't going to go to school right now.

Beverly was strong enough and convincing enough to let me know that I was wrong and that I was going to school right now. I started school just like I was told (smile). I still have to consummate one fourth level French course to complete the requirements for my Bachelor of Arts in Psychology. The bulk of the work has been done and it is just a matter of going through the formalities for me.

My Beverly, upon my release, was incessantly spouting avowals of her love for the Lord. I loved her and yet I felt scorned. I had no understanding of how this Holy Ghost stuff would or should have any effect on us getting married. God was not a real thing to me that way. To me, there was reality and then, on the other hand, there was God. To Beverly, God was her entire reality. She had changed, but there was also an underlying sentiment that was pressing against my thoughts at the same time. She had exceeded every criterion that I ever imagined relating to how I could know that somebody loved me. She had done that and more. She had prostrated her entire life for me. She was committed, faithful and unwavering. She was vigilant.

This was the woman that I believed I was made to love. She answered all the questions that opined deep in my heart. I loved her and then some.

I knew that she loved me in every way that I could define the term, but yet she would not marry me because of this Holy Ghost stuff. She was pursuing the things of God and I was just a thorn in her side. We had close communication until October 1977. When our relationship reached the point where we recognized that we would not be together, I began spending all of my time with my sons' mother. She enabled and complemented my thug life. We were married in October 1977. This final cut of the umbilical cord between Beverly and I was because of her respect for the sanctity of the marriage union. Beverly cut off all contact.

By now, I had a heroin habit again. I was involved with some thugs in an organized crime environment. We sold drugs; we did a lot of other things on the side – robbery, prostitution, whatever we thought that we could do to get money. Some among the group were doing much better financially than others. We looked the role – we drove big cars and dressed well. It was the way that we lived. Beverly was out of my life at this point. In 1983 my sons mother and I broke up. I walked out. I went back to my mother's house temporarily and somehow Beverly and I established phone contact temporarily. She was more mature in the things of God.

In the following ninety days, the paths of our lives crossed. She recommended that I attend a service at a church near my mother's house. I went to Word of Faith church at her suggestion. I was not actively using drugs for a period of months during this time. I was working construction as a contractor . It was during that time that I met the woman who became my second wife.

We met at church. She was a convenient enabler and quite a carnal baby Christian just as I was. Here I was, in the church not using drugs right then, and here was this convenient woman.

Before long, I saw that I was not going to be able to make it with Beverly like this, so I just dropped out of her life again. She had a good life. She was working as a teacher and prospering well. She even had a beautiful apartment on the lake. I loved her. I knew it, but I recognized my incapacity and knew I had to move on. I did not fully recognize the bondage that the power of sin still had over my life.

I got married a second time and my contact with "My Beverly" was broken again in 1983. I lived with this woman unmarried for three years. We bought a house together. She had children from a previous marriage. My drug use escalated. I was working as an apprentice millwright out of the union hall making an average of $1,000 a week. My drug use progressively escalated and this poor woman suffered with a very mature, deeply rooted dope fiend thug wannabe poorly disguised as a husband. She was a good woman. She was a professional accountant for Chrysler Corp. She

149

eventually became an attorney.

Yet, she had an enabling character about her and our carnal spirits suited each other as we went on together. I brought a lot of pain and suffering into her and her three children's lives. It is a painful thing to think about. One of the best things that happened to her was in January 1989 when I was in the car accident that I mentioned earlier. I was working out of the union hall on a project in Midland, Michigan. They said that I was driving a truck that hit a guardrail, flipped over and threw me out. It broke my neck in three placcs and my leg in five places. I had to undergo numerous surgeries, and as I mentioned earlier, they told me that I died on the operating table on at least one occasion. I suffered extreme injuries.

For the next five years, I could not work. I collected social security disability. I was receiving $4,000 a month that was usually consumed before the end of each month by a $200 a day dope habit. In fact, it was not long after the accident that I received the first check for $26,000. I gave her about $5,000 and left the home we shared. I went back to my mother's house and she divorced me. I was temporarily a dope fiend that could support my habit.

My mother was still there for me. My mother was just a mother; all she knew was that she loved her son and that she had money to help. I paid no rent, but I would still have to borrow money from my parents by the end of every month. I was also addicted to a high dosage of methadone. I was smoking crack and shooting eight $25 packs of dope every day. I was passing out daily under the influence of these drugs. Knowing that I frequently passed out, I would pay people to ride in the car with me to make sure that I wasn't robbed while I was unconscious. I became accustomed to passing out. This is how I lived until the money ran out.

When the money ran out, I was reduced to receiving a $600 disability check once a month. I went from living high on the hog to living in squalor. I moved to the north end of Detroit and lived like a dope fiend on less than $1,000 a month. I had an apartment in a building where everyone was like me (i.e., a destitute drug addict). I remember this one man who was a loan shark. He would loan money at the rate of a dollar for a dollar - 100% interest! He would wait at the mailbox on check day with a bat.

I went through this period just prior to meeting Pastor Jackson in Monroe. I reconnected with my second wife and we had a short stint. I believe that her interest in me was money-related because when she found out that I couldn't contribute to her needs, she dumped me. I can't blame her for that.

That was in 1990. I tried to go back to work as a millwright in 1993, but it was too physically challenging. My body just couldn't take it, so I went back to the streets and I almost got killed. I was in halo traction after the third operation on my spinal cord. In 1993, they performed a second bone fusion where they again took a bone fragment from my pelvis and put it into the cervical area of my spine.

I believe I probably broke my own neck while I was high. I never told people this, but I believe that I did the damage to myself. I had such excruciating pain when I regained consciousness from an overdose. I was in such pain that I had to go back to the hospital. The doctors determined that the first bone fusion had come apart, so they went in again.

151

The second time that they went in they had to enter my spinal cord through the front of my neck. That is the reason why I have this big scar on my throat. Entering my spinal cord from the front, they believed that during the process I got infected. But personally I suspect that that was not the case. I had been shooting dope in the Brewster projects following the second surgery. A resourceful dope fiend had climbed the utility pole and turned on the electricity in an abandoned building. He wired the building himself. It was cold that night and I remember being downtown after being released from the hospital.

I had some dope and I was trying to get a hit. I remember that I had to lie down so someone could hit me because I couldn't find a vein. I paid someone to hit me in my jugular vein.

I believe I got infected during that hit in the dirty environment of that dimly lit abandoned building. The area near the stitches was not fully healed. Anyway, the pain became so excruciating within a few days that I went back to the hospital. They took me through emergency immediately. They told me that I had an infection that had to be drained immediately. This was the third time that I had surgery on my spinal cord. I was on life support for eleven days. I was told that I died during that operation also. When I finally recovered, I was partially paralyzed. I couldn't touch my baby finger and my thumb on either hand. It took me a number of months in the hospital undergoing physical therapy before I was able to perform that simple gesture.

It was following this third operation that they put me into halo traction. It is a big device that was screwed into my skull. I was discharged. My mother helped me get a room at a hotel.

While living there, I had to ask my mother to bring me $80 because I smoked up a dope man's money. He gave me some crack to sell, but instead, I smoked it. He was going to kill me for $80. I was already in halo traction, but he was going to finish me off if I didn't get that money to him that day. I will always remember the look on my mother and sisters faces as they walked away after bringing me the money to that hotel lobby. It was a horrible time; a very bad time.

Things continued to happen to me as I went through the revolving doors of treatment centers. It got worse. I somehow was able to get a job through the union hall making $800 a week in 1994. I was able to balance my dope habit financially for some months by joining the methadone clinic. Methadone therapy minimized my need to chase heroin as vigorously. I rented a house and bought a car. To a casual observer, I would appear almost socially acceptable. I was going through the motions, but it didn't last very long. I think I stayed on that job for eight or nine months. I eventually lost the job because the dope habit always increases disproportionately to everything else in a dope fiends life.

I couldn't sustain the juggling act. I was spending about $100 a week on methadone. I was smoking $50-$100 a day in crack and drinking about $20-$30 a day in alcohol. Whatever happened to me on a given day, just happened! I just didn't care.

Before I leave this time period, between 1995 and 1997, let me say again that I was kicked out of every treatment center that I ever went to. The Cass Corridor area was about the only place that I knew to go to since I didn't have any friends or money. I did the revolving door thing with all of the different treatment centers. I eventually ended up sitting in the chairs at the NSO. In 1997, this is where God found me and where He has brought me from.

After my release from the treatment center in 1997, I went back to work at the union hall. My first assignment was at a Ford /Mazda plant in Flat Rock, Michigan. I was earning over a $1,000 a week. I was free from drugs and I knew it. I was walking in that freedom as best I understood. I had not, however, connected myself with a church home yet.

I began working with a church ministry at the NSO. I was doing evangelist outreach. In my private life, I was searching to find my place in Him. I knew that this was the place where I wanted to stay - where I belonged. I knew I was free. I wanted to learn about my freedom - how He did what He had done for me. I wanted to know what I could do for Him. This went on for about a year. I saved my money and with it I started COMAYA Ministries by feeding street people. Another ministry voluntarily supplied me with enough food to continue feeding people on the streets. We still feed people.

But even amid overwhelming thoughts of how I had been miraculously brought from slavery to deliverance, I could never forget my Beverly. I knew that my love, Beverly, had been used by God to start all of this. After all, the mother of my sons had been introduced to the word of Christ and received the baptism of the Holy Ghost after being led to the Lord by Beverly. We were not married only because Beverly would not forsake the commandment of God. Beverly helped the woman that I married get the Holy Ghost. This was quite a traumatic event precisely when Beverly's contact in my life was becoming increasingly minimal.

At the same time that God was becoming more prominent in Beverly's life, I had been drawn back into the lifestyle from which I had come. I was in search of my own heart. I had an apartment in Highland Park. For nearly a year, I was ashamed to even think about Beverly. I had taken her through so much. I had hurt her so much, so many times. There was so much drama associated with my life that I was ashamed to even dwell on thoughts of Beverly. But yet the memory of her I knew would never go away.

I had heard from my mother that Beverly was married in 1989. While she was getting married, I was in a hospital in her hometown at death's door on the operating table. She was married just after my life almost ended from the car accident. I was ashamed to think of her ever being a part of my life again. But there was another part of me still grieving the loss of the love of my life deep in my heart. Maybe it was only a feeling, but I could not live without trying.

I bought three cards. My conscious mind said that I wanted to at least let her know that I had made it to Jesus and I just wanted to thank her, but my heart was saying something else. I bought these three cards and I carried them for months in my tote bag. I wrote these three thank you notes and I signed them. I was under the impression that she was married and that she had gone on with her life. I had no direct means of contacting her. My mother told me something about her living on the waterfront in downtown Detroit. I checked with all the waterfront housing units, but nobody knew anything.

Finally, I remembered the street name where her mother lived in Flint. For months, I had these three cards that I carried around. One Sunday, I called to make inquiry about a car. I

155

wanted to buy a Mercedes, but I had heard about this good looking Jaguar. I thought maybe I could make a deal with the owner. This particular Sunday morning, I was also on my way to visit a new church for the first time. I knew the location, but I exited the freeway at the wrong exit. Now that I was late, I decided to go and find out about the car, so I called the man about the Jaguar. His price was so high that I abandoned the idea.

The thought suddenly occurred to me to take these cards to Beverly's mother in Flint. It is about an hour's drive from Detroit. Arriving at her mother's door unannounced after so many years, I knew I would have to tell her something real convincing to justify my visit. So I went to Flint and I had to search to find the house. I remembered the street, but I didn't have the correct address. I went around the corner to a church service. At the end of the service, I went back and began asking the neighbors. They told me the correct address. I was on the right street, but had gone to the wrong house. I was close.

I went to the door and I spoke with her mother. After greetings, I told her why I was there with the cards and asked her to give them to Beverly. I asked how Beverly was doing. She said fine. When I was getting ready to leave, I told her that I knew that she had heard all of these things through the media about women that fell in love with men in prison. She must have heard what fools these women were said to be. I told her mother that I wanted her to know that her daughter was not a fool and that I loved her daughter with everything that I had. I told her mother that our love was pure and Beverly should never be thought of as anybody's fool. I wanted her to know that her daughter was an honorable lady.

When I stood up to walk out the door, her mother told me that she would be sure to tell Beverly what I had said. She then somehow mentioned that Beverly was divorced. Uh oh! She told me that the man she married was a nice guy, but they just couldn't make it work. Beverly had been divorced for three years. I asked her mother if she could tell me where Beverly was. She told me that she was working in the school system in Detroit. I thanked her, but in my mind, I knew that my mission would be to find her. I knew that she was going to be mine, period! That is what I call her today - "Mine."

My new mission was to get my baby back. I found out that she was working at a middle school on the east side. I visited the school I went to as a kid. I contacted the school and it just so happened that Albert was the head boiler operator at the school. Albert and I went to this very same school years before as children. I told him my story and told him that all I knew was her maiden name. I just wanted to know anyone with the name of Beverly. I didn't know that I was only blocks away from the right school.

I went to the school center building, the headquarters for the Detroit Public School System. There were two women by the name of Beverly. I called the first name. A woman answered, but I knew that wasn't her. The second number I called was an answering machine, but I knew that it was Beverly's voice. I said ok and I left a voice mail message. I kept leaving voice mails for weeks and weeks. I kept trying to contact her. I remembered how close her and my mother had been. I went to my mother and pleaded my case. My mother even knew that I was ready. She called the number I gave her and left a message for Beverly. Finally, we were able to talk.

I heard her voice. She tells people that I told her in our first conversation that I wanted to marry her. I was so happy I can't remember. All I know is that I was ashamed, but I was not shy. I have loved her all of my life. I was looking for her even in the part of my life when I didn't know how to love her. During both of my marriages, both ex-wives knew that I loved Beverly. My sons' mother, of course, had contact with her and knew her. She accepted that I loved Beverly, but my second wife was always haunted by images of Beverly. She met Beverly, but only had minor contact with her. Her belief was that Beverly was so spiritually alienated from me that even though I did love Beverly, it wouldn't really count as a violation to our union. These two women accepted me despite my love for Beverly.

It didn't take me long to tell her what I wanted. It is amazing when I look at it now. Again, she did the comaya - come as you are. She accepted me just as I was. I have been changing and, hopefully, I am getting better. Beverly accepted me. I didn't know or care what kind of circumstance that I might find her in. All I knew was that if she was alive, I wanted her to know that I loved her and that I have always loved her. I wanted her to know that she is mine, period! I was prepared to resort to whatever means were necessary. And believe me, she took me through some things, but I didn't care.

I didn't care who was in her life. I was obsessed enough to even think that I could employ thug life activities to get my woman back. I won't go into any details, but it doesn't take a whole lot of imagination to understand that no human being, especially a man, was going to stop me. I was prepared to have honored her marriage vows, though. Had her mother not told me that she was divorced, I was prepared to leave and accept it. While it had hurt me just to know that she was married, all other considerations were canceled when I heard that she was divorced. She would be mine again.

And she has been mine ever since. It was not an easy journey. It was a year of screening by her before she agreed to marry me. We were married on June 26, 1999. That date marks another chapter of the ongoing saga of Beverly and Allen. We are now spiritually on the same page. We are not on the same line or paragraph. We are not equals. I appreciate her and respect her walk following the Lord for all these years. It has been over thirty years. I do not try to compare myself to her. I just try to love her real good. My heart is set on knowing that I have been a positive contribution to her life. If nothing else, she knows that she is loved by this man who loves her with everything that I have. She is my love, my life: "My Beverly."

Chapter 18: *Grover*

If in describing the events that happened in my life I sound like I am bragging, I apologize. This will only occur due to my careless and unintentional failure to communicate. Allow me to emphasize the fact that I take no pride in the life that I lived before Christ. It was shamefully disgusting. I was caught up, hopelessly entangled and truly a slave.

By the end of my bondage period, I was completely out of control. The momentum was devastating and I, therefore, have absolutely nothing to be proud of. But I feel the need to raise this issue since I have even recognized in reviewing the manuscript how sometimes I almost sound like I am glorying in my past shame. Let me assure the reader that there was but one thing in this story to brag about: Jesus and the mercy He extended to a fool like me. This is all that I can humbly boast about.

My life was horribly miserable with an occasional bright spot due to twisted notions about some things thought of as fun at the time. Sometimes when talking about my past, I unconsciously assume a tone in my expression as if I was there again. I will also be careful not to mention details of other crimes that I was either involved in or know about. In most cases, these crimes involved accomplices and carried sentences for which there is no statute of limitations.

While in the midst of my bondage, in my heart, I always hoped to someday be a kind of spokesperson. I dreamed of being the voice of the hopeless addicts who wouldn't live to express their true feelings to the world.

This hope burned inside of me as it does with so many slaves. It was not until the very end when all hope was gone that I abandoned that dream. I finally abandoned any hope that this day would ever come. But God had another plan. I now have faith in my God and my Beverly.

This chapter in my life addresses one very personal reason why I am writing this book. There once was a man who crossed the path of my life that I will never forget. His name was Grover. As stated earlier, I grew up on the east side of Detroit. My family came to Detroit in 1955. The neighborhood that I lived in was adjacent to a neighborhood called the "Black Bottom." My high school was located in the Black Bottom. There was a lot of gang activity during the early 1960's. Black Bottom was a black community that was economically and socially considered the bottom of the barrel - hard core poverty. Grover and I lived near each other just north of the Black Bottom. A railroad track divided our communities.

As a young child, I could not go into Grover's neighborhood because of the gangs, but as a teenager, some of us would venture into other neighborhoods for parties and to chase girls. I had a relationship with a lot of people in that general area by the time I was a teenager. Many of us attended the same high school. I could move freely between the different groups because I was never part of any gang. I thought of myself as being above that. My thinking, of course, was just a foolish notion that I embraced. I was appropriately thought of as a real threat to nobody.

Grover and I never met growing up. We first met in Jackson Prison after I had been sentenced to life in 1971. We were

161

both twenty-one years old. Because of my age, I had to sign a waiver to go inside the walls of Jackson. It was required of convicts to be at least twenty-two to go inside the walls as I have mentioned before. Jackson Prison was the institution that reputedly held the hardest of the hard and the toughest of the tough in Michigan. A waiver relieved the Michigan Department of Corrections of responsibility for whatever happened to me. I signed the waiver.

My thinking at the time was that if I had to go to Ionia (a youth prison for people doing long sentences), I would have to gain my respect twice. I figured since I knew I would have to trail blaze and do what was necessary to get my respect in prison, I would prefer to do it once and for all. If I went to Ionia because of my long sentence, I would still have to go to Jackson anyway.

I chose to go inside the walls of Jackson. At that time, prisoners from various neighborhoods freely communicated during yard period. Grover and I had attended the same high school, but he had dropped out. We knew some of the same people. I was hanging out inside the walls with a guy named Richard P. He was in there for murder and rape. I believe Richard P. had something to do with me getting hit in the head with a pipe six days after I was inside the walls, but I never learned the details. I heard that the guy that I was walking with was actually the target. I also heard that somebody had assigned this guy to attack us. They were testing us to see if we were soft. If we broke following the attack, then we'd be prime candidates to be girls for the duration of our sentence.

Anyway, I knew Richard P. from our neighborhood. R.P. retaliated against the guy who hit me and also the guy that was walking with me. I am not sure if R.P's motives were that honorable because he was a known rapist himself. He may have been involved in a scheme to set-up one or both of us. All I know is that I met Grover in the process of knowing R.P. since they hung out in the same gang on the streets. R.P. was called hatchet man because he used to fight with a hatchet. He is dead now. He did some bad and crazy stuff before and after his release.

Anyway, Grover and I developed a relationship. He had respect for me as a gang leader. We had a click that we called the family. I was the war lord. Again, we stood about seventy-five strong inside the walls of Jackson. We gained respect through the power of our numbers. We were not involved in a lot of organized money making ventures. Mainly, we stayed together for strength. People knew that if you dealt with one of the family, you dealt with all of the family.

Grover did errands for me and carried messages. He worked for us helping to extort money from people. He was a good gopher. He would not, however, commit violence against anyone. (He was serving a five to fifteen year sentence for armed robbery.) He was like many guys that were vacuumed by the momentum of their childhood neighborhood. He had gone along with the crew and participated in a robbery. After our time together in Jackson, over ten years elapsed before our next meeting. I was released from Jackson in 1975 on an appeal bond. I ultimately pleaded no contest to 2nd degree murder and I was given five to fifteen with time served and two years parole.

My parole was in Ann Arbor, so I moved back and forth between Detroit and Ann Arbor. As my involvement with drugs and crime progressed, I ended up more in Detroit than Ann Arbor. I reconnected with the drug business through my associations from prison. A guy named Shug set me up with my first half quarter of dope.

Upon receiving the money for the first sale, I went back to get more dope from Shug, but he had been killed. He was shot eighteen times while leaving his dope house.

The shooter was one of our childhood playmates. He was set-up by a guy who was supposed to be part of our crew. But Shug didn't die from the gun shots. He died from a heart attack. He had gained a lot of weight over the years. The shooters cut his finger off to take his diamond ring. They also took the $18,000 out of his pocket. It was a mess.

I was dealing now and I had some contacts around downtown Detroit. I ran into Grover and he did some work around town for me. I liked Grover. I was struggling to support a bad dope habit. I was back to work as a millwright after a four year break due to a car accident. I was making over $1,000 a week, but had developed a heroin habit expense of $100 a day. I was also drinking about a pint a day. If any money was left, I would use it to smoke crack until I passed out.

At some point, I was fired for threatening my supervisor. This particular supervisor was actually one of the few friends I still had on the job. In a drunken rage, I cursed him out and threatened him publicly. To my undoing, his supervisor heard me threaten him and made him lay me off. But my reputation as a hard worker was good enough that my reputation for drinking and drugging was overlooked. I was hardly ever denied placement on a job assignment since there was so much drinking and drugging going on among the craftsman. If you were good and had connections, then you could normally work.

In 1995, my dope habit was so out of control that the general foreman had to get rid of me to save his own job. He got rid of me and I went to two other little shop jobs just to keep making money. But my drug habit had got so bad that I just could not work. I had rented a house on a street where my two sons hung out. They were teenagers at the time. They ultimately suffered, before their friends , embarrassment and shame because of me. At one point, I had three cars in my driveway. But within weeks, along with my rented house, I lost everything. I was evicted having all my belongings set on the streets. I lost all of my furniture and my clothes. I lost everything and I moved back to my mother's house.

I resorted to doing anything to support my habit. I sold my best car for $100, but it was worth over $1,000. One of my cars was hot. I left that in the driveway. One car I gave to a guy that I had paid to fix it. I was walking. I couldn't work. The only thing that I had was a dope habit and even my mother couldn't afford that. That was the last time I stayed at my mother's house before my deliverance.

I remember on one occasion poking around the house while no one was there , looking for something that I could sell to buy a dose of heroin. I needed a "blow." A dose of heroin cost $10. I couldn't find anything but her penny piggy bank, so I got enough money from pop bottles and the penny piggy bank to get some dope. When I got back, she had noticed some disruption in her penny piggy bank. She asked me about it and I denied it. I can still remember her telling me that though she knew that I did it, she needed me to admit what I did. I couldn't and I didn't.

Soon after that, she told me that she loved me, but she couldn't stand to see me like I was and that she couldn't afford to be around me. I was trusted in my parents' home only while escorted by a family member. I couldn't sleep there anymore. So, I left one night after stealing her TV. I only returned over a year later after my deliverance.

I went to the Cass Corridor - the walk-in center. At this homeless shelter, anybody can just walk in and sit in a chair. If you don't bother anyone, nobody will bother you for the rest of your life. During winter, the walk-in center networked with other shelters that would provide a meal and a warm place to sleep. One of the warming centers was the Brewster Center. At the Brewster Center, I went through the required ritual of taking a shower. We were then given a meal and a cot in a large gym area. Each morning they gave us a snack. We then would have to leave until that evening.

It was here that I ran into Grover again. He was homeless too. Grover had suffered kidney failure and was taking dialysis treatments three times a week. He was probably a diabetic also. He was taking pills and other medications as well. He said he had to eat in the morning on the days of his dialysis. Though he was dependent upon the Brewster Shelter like I was, he still owned a van, but had no money to keep it running. He parked his van outside the Brewster Center in the employee lot. The shelter policy was that if a homeless person failed to arrive at the shelter by a certain time you couldn't come in. So, Grover would sleep in his van when he couldn't make it to the shelter in time. He kept blankets in the van to keep him warm.

The morning after we met at the shelter, they gave us our snack and we left at 5:30 a.m. It was still very cold and dark. Both of us understood that we would be looking for a way to get some dope. Grover would also be scheming to come up with enough money to get some food before his dialysis. We went to sit in his van. It was cold and the blankets really helped. We heard a little sound and he told me that there was a rat in the van. I asked him why he didn't get it out and he said, "I don't have anything to get it out with." I asked what are we doing in here with a rat and he answered quite frankly that we were staying out of the cold. I only stayed with him that one time.

We stayed for a couple of hours until it was light outside. Then, we were off to make a hustle to get a blow and something to eat. I saw him around the Cass Corridor a few more times over the months. Then, some months elapsed before I saw him again. Once again, I started seeing him regularly as we both chased crack in the Cass Corridor. I heard that the dope boys were using his room to sell crack. Those were my last casual contacts with Grover.

The next time I heard anything about Grover, I was told that he had met his demise in an alley. Some guys had beat him up and left him to die there. They brutally beat him to death in that alley. To relate this story is very hard. With tears as I write and with sorrow in my heart, I know that I will always remember Grover. I was close enough to Grover to know what I believe was in his heart. He really was a good person.

He was really a nice guy. He wasn't violent like I was. He would do what we told him to do. He participated in some illegal things with other people, but he never initiated violence.

When there was a conflict down in the dope world, Grover would always be the peace maker. He would tell me things about his family and his childhood: about his mother - private and hurtful things that I don't believe he could tell a lot of people. Even though I was a dope addict like him, I grieve in my heart over the circumstances of his death. I told Grover that if I ever lived to get out of this place (dope life) alive (I knew that I was a slave to dope just like he was) I was going to tell people about him. I would tell people that he was not just a dope addict; that he had a heart and that he loved his mama. He wanted to do right, but he was bound by something he didn't understand.

I knew back then that Grover represented a whole group of people that would never be heard. I always believed, until the very end of my addiction, that I would live to be the voice of all the dead and silent Grovers in this world. It is only by the grace and mercy of God that I have made it here. Somebody will hear their story - their silent outcry from the grave - even if it is just my Beverly.

Grover was just a little insignificant bug of a man in the eyes of the world, but he had a heart. He loved and he hurt. I can't speak for everybody, but I know there were a lot of Grovers around me shooting that dope, drinking that alcohol and smoking crack. I knew them, they knew me and many of them opened up their hearts to me. Why? I don't know; maybe for such a time as this.

I didn't want to write this book. I didn't think that this would be a suitable forum to express the heart of a slave from the mouth of a former slave. Like so many others, I didn't even believe that there existed a way out of bondage. But I do know now. His name is Jesus. That is another reason why I wrote this book. For all the Grovers of the world, unto the glory of God, I am indebted. And just as the Lord has manifested a glimpse of His glory in my life, I stand firmly as a living testimony that Jesus loves you just because He loves you.

EPILOGUE

As Allen's wife, there is no one closer to his heart than I am. I must say that I was nothing less than astounded at reading about a man who has the same fingerprints as my Allen, yet is nothing like him. The Allen I know is an extreme contrast to the individual depicted in his book.

My Allen has the heart of God since he accepted Jesus as the Lord of his life. He is a gentle, loving, caring, and compassionate person. Allen feels so deeply, that he cries very easily. I believe that he would solve every human being's problems on the planet if it were possible.

As my husband, Allen treats me as if God only created one female. He is a wonderful, hardworking provider, a fun loving companion and my best friend. Allen never tires of reading the Bible and praising God. He spends a great deal of time in prayer.

Allen's old life consisted of an inordinate desire to acquire wealth predominately to support his substance abuse addiction. No crime was too inhumane to accomplish this. He was considered an irresponsible homeless bum as well as a loathsome, psychopathic criminal.

The mighty power of God is truly demonstrated in the rebirth of Allen Bennett, Jr. Allen's intelligence as an honor student from the University of Michigan is no longer being used for ill repute. He is a successful Millwright Journeyman for Chrysler Corporation as well as a real estate owner of several properties.

His earnest desire is to assist everyone he can in receiving the Mighty One (Jesus) who delivered him from a life of a living hell. He is convinced that only then can a person be free of unnecessary pain, guilt and bondage. Because I feel the same way, Allen and I are extremely happy.

Though the material gain God has blessed us with has been a miraculous turn around for Allen, what we enjoy most is growing in God together. Allen has learned before it was too late that the Light of Christ is definitely the best path to follow forever. He literally has been born again.

About the Author
Allen Bennett

- ☐ I died on the operating table a few times
- ☐ I overdosed countless times
- ☐ A police hit squad was hired to kill me
- ☐ I knowingly shot strychnine poison into my own veins
- ☐ Why did the Lord spare my stupid life?
- ☐ Why did He let me live to write this book?
- ☐ Why do I get to live comfortably with my lovely wife?

Nearly everyone who lived the street life with me is either dead, walking the streets out of their mind, incarcerated, a fugitive from justice or in a mental institution. Why am I here?

Can Jesus deliver an arrogant dope fiend, convicted robber, murderer, drug dealer wannabe; a selfish Detroit hustler who feared nothing and cared for no one? YES! In one day.

I am the dead man that lives in Detroit

To order additional copies of this contact:

Allen Bennett
E-mail: beruandal@aol.com

www.ingramcontent.com/pod-product-compliance
Lightning Source LLC
Chambersburg PA
CBHW031845090426

42741CB00005B/365